T0286788

Cambridge Elements ≡

Elements in Shakespeare and Text
edited by
Claire M. L. Bourne
The Pennsylvania State University
Rory Loughnane
University of Kent

FACSIMILES AND THE HISTORY OF SHAKESPEARE EDITING

Paul Salzman
La Trobe University

CAMBRIDGE
UNIVERSITY PRESS

CAMBRIDGE
UNIVERSITY PRESS

Shaftesbury Road, Cambridge CB2 8EA, United Kingdom

One Liberty Plaza, 20th Floor, New York, NY 10006, USA

477 Williamstown Road, Port Melbourne, VIC 3207, Australia

314–321, 3rd Floor, Plot 3, Splendor Forum, Jasola District Centre,
New Delhi – 110025, India

103 Penang Road, #05–06/07, Visioncrest Commercial, Singapore 238467

Cambridge University Press is part of Cambridge University Press & Assessment,
a department of the University of Cambridge.

We share the University's mission to contribute to society through the pursuit of
education, learning and research at the highest international levels of excellence.

www.cambridge.org
Information on this title: www.cambridge.org/9781009228244

DOI: 10.1017/9781009228268

First published 2023

A catalogue record for this publication is available from the British Library.

ISBN 978-1-009-22824-4 Paperback
ISSN 2754-4257 (online)
ISSN 2754-4249 (print)

Facsimiles and the History of Shakespeare Editing

Elements in Shakespeare and Text

DOI: 10.1017/9781009228268

First published online: March 2023

Paul Salzman

La Trobe University

Author for correspondence: Paul Salzman, P.Salzman@latrobe.edu.au

ABSTRACT: Is a facsimile an edition? In answering this question in relation to Shakespeare and to early modern writing in general, the author explores the interrelationship between the beginning of the conventional process of collecting and editing Shakespeare's plays and the increasing sophistication of facsimiles. While recent scholarship has offered a detailed account of how Shakespeare was edited in the eighteenth century, the parallel process of the 'exact' reproduction of his texts has been largely ignored. The author will explain how facsimiles moved during the eighteenth and nineteenth centuries from hand-drawn, traced, and type-facsimiles to the advent of photographical facsimiles in the mid-nineteenth century. Facsimiles can be seen as a barometer of the reverence accorded to the idea of an authentic Shakespeare text, and also of the desire to possess, if not original texts, then their reproductions.

KEYWORDS: Shakespeare, facsimiles, editing, digital reproduction, literary history

ISBNs: 9781009228244 (PB), 9781009228268 (OC)

ISSNs: 2754-4257 (online), 2754-4249 (print)

Contents

Introduction: What Is a Facsimile and Why Does It Matter?

In his short story 'Pierre Menard, Author of the *Quixote*', Jorge Luis Borges, assuming the narrative voice of an academic pedant, describes how the writer Pierre Menard sets out, not to copy, but to produce 'word for word and line for line', a portion of Cervantes's *Don Quixote*.[1] Menard succeeds, but then the narrator explains that, because of the passage of time (although this is not exactly how he describes the situation), Menard's *Quixote* is completely different in meaning to Cervantes's, even though the words are identical. This little fable illustrates perfectly the paradox of the facsimile which I will be exploring in this Element. A facsimile is intended to be a replica rather than a copy; facsimiles reproduce the form of a text rather than just the content. If 'facsimile' literally means making something that is the same as something else, then the slippery status of the facsimile occurs because of the act of making – a slipperiness also indicated by the slippage between 'similis', meaning alike or merely similar. Like Menard's *Quixote*, the facsimile of an early modern text is both identical and different: the closer one looks, and the more one takes into account the context of a particular facsimile, the more differences appear, even when at first glance the replica seems identical to the original.

In this Element, I argue that the rise in the number and quality of facsimiles coincided with the rise in formal editorial activity centred on Shakespeare in the eighteenth and nineteenth centuries, but extended to other early modern (and classical) texts. Throughout, I contend that a facsimile is different from a forgery, though the two are not unrelated. On the flip side, many a facsimile has also been mistaken for an 'original'. Through exploring this history, I will also cast light on current interest in the affordances and drawbacks of modern digital reproductions of early modern texts (often referred to as 'digital facsimiles'), especially of Shakespeare's texts.

Because this Element focusses on Shakespeare and associated authors, I will be concentrating on facsimiles of printed texts, rather than manuscripts, though there will be some crossovers between the two. In historicizing the

---

[1] Jorge Louis Borges, 'Pierre Menard, Author of the *Quixote*', trans. Anthony Bonner, *Ficciones* (New York: Grove Press, 1962), 45–55.

facsimile, I am taking my cue from the consideration of textual reproduction in David McKitterick's excellent, wide-ranging study *Old Books, New Technologies*.[2] McKitterick sees facsimiles as part of the way antiquarian books have been used and reused, within the context of what could be termed 'historical bibliography'. He outlines the development from what I would term 'artisanal facsimiles', whether drawn, traced, or printed with old type or pseudo-old type, through to the technological innovations of photographic and then digital reproduction. In this study, I contend that there are significant correlations between changes in approach to the editing of Shakespeare and the use of facsimiles as a mode of transmitting and permitting wider access to copies of early texts. Like McKitterick, I explore how a historical approach to the facsimile – one that understands it as related to other forms of textual production and reproduction – speaks to current debates about the nature and effectiveness of digital reproductions of early modern books, though I will be arguing for more of a balance between the positive and negative impact of the digital turn.[3]

As a prelude to a brief history of facsimiles, I want to begin with a particularly illuminating case history, which might be called 'The Case of the Facsimile That Kept Fooling People'. Here, side by side, are the title pages of a 1599 play usually attributed to Thomas Kyd, printed in quarto, entitled *Solimon and Perseda* (Figure 1).

The page on the left is the title page as printed in 1599, while the page on the right is of a facsimile dating from around 1805. This is specifically a type-facsimile produced by the printer Joseph Smeeton. This kind of facsimile can be contrasted with those that were traced or hand-drawn, sometimes referred to as pen-facsimiles.[4] Traced facsimiles tended to be of single pages, done in order to supply what was missing from a genuine early modern book. Here, for example, is the traced final page of Shakespeare's

[2] David McKitterick, *Old Books, New Technologies: The Representation, Conservation and Transformation of Books since 1700* (Cambridge: Cambridge University Press, 2013).

[3] See ibid., pp. 211–13.

[4] For more details about different kinds of facsimiles, see the Glossary.

Figure 1 Title pages of *Solimon and Perseda*, Harry Ransom Center, Pforz 953, Pforz 953 PFZ

first folio, done by the most famous of all nineteenth-century practitioners of this art, John Harris (Figure 2A).[5]

If you look very closely beneath the elaborate final ornament, you can see that Harris has signed his work (Figure 2B).[6]

---

[5] I do not use capitals for Shakespeare's first folio given that this is a descriptive term, not the title of the book.

[6] On Harris see especially Sarah Werner's excellent Folger Shakespeare Library 'Collation' entry, 'Pen Facsimiles of Early Print' (https://collation.folger. edu/2013/05/pen-facsimiles-of-early-print, accessed 11 December 2021), and McKitterick, *Old Books, New Technologies*, pp. 105–8.

Figure 2A Final traced page of first folio, Folger Shakespeare Library STC 22273 fo. 1 no. 23

Figure 2B

Harris was the most acclaimed practitioner of this specialized art in the nineteenth century, and I will discuss his work in more detail in Section 2. Here I just want to note the paradox that Harris's pen-work produces an extremely accurate facsimile of a printed page, albeit one deliberately signed so you know that what you see is not the original.

In contrast, a type-facsimile like *Solimon and Perseda*, where the apparent replication of the actual process of early modern printing is a less exact reproduction because it uses type like but not identical to the original, was still capable of fooling people. Joseph Smeeton, who produced the early nineteenth-century type-facsimile of Kyd's play, belonged to a dynasty of printers, with his printing shop responsible for far more than just facsimiles.[7] The more closely one examines Smeeton's facsimile of *Solimon and Perseda*, the more departures from the original become

---

[7] All of Smeeton's work is signed 'J. Smeeton', which has perhaps led to some confusion. A. T. Hazen suggests the printer was a John Smeeton ('Type-Facsimiles', *MP* 64 (1947), pp. 209–17, at p. 209). In fact, as David McKitterick notes, Joseph Smeeton and his son George were printers in St Martins Lane, and Joseph was certainly responsible for the *Solimon and Perseda* facsimile; see McKitterick, *Old Books, New Technologies*, p. 88. The date of the facsimile is hard to determine, but given that Joseph died in a fire at the print shop in 1809, with George carrying on the printing work, the facsimile has to have been printed earlier, possibly around 1805 (see British Book Trade Index, Smeeton, Joseph, bbti.bodleian.ox.ac.uk, accessed 23 February 2020).

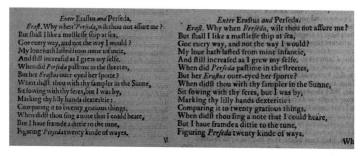

Figure 3 Comparison of original and facsimile, Harry Ransom Center,
Pforz 953, Pforz 953 PFZ

apparent – but only, of course, if an original is available for the comparison. This is the kind of type-facsimile where the printer has not used remaining examples of the original type, but rather has used type that closely resembles the original. In this instance, it appears that Smeeton used a Caslon typeface designed by William Caslon in 1722. The differences become apparent when the original and the facsimile are placed side by side and examined line by line. This is more obvious with the typeface than with the printer's ornaments, such as the one on the title page, where the ornaments were almost certainly traced from the printed original and then made into woodblocks.[8] For example, the type that Smeeton used did not contain the same italic capital E used for the character name Erastus, as we can see when the examples are placed next to each other (see Figure 3).

A similar example can be found on the final page, where once again the type cannot be matched exactly, so the last word, 'Finis', has a swash capital in the original and a plain capital in the facsimile.

It is difficult to know whether Smeeton intended his facsimile to deceive people into believing they were looking at an original; like Harris, Smeeton signed his work, but, unlike Harris, he left his mark in a spot (at the very

---

[8] The title page fleuron is in Henry R. Plomer, *English Printers' Ornaments* (London: Grafton & Company, 1924), No. 93.

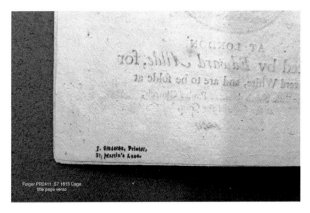

Figure 4 Facsimile title page verso, Folger Shakespeare Library

bottom of the verso of the title page) where it might easily be cut away without leaving much evidence that it had ever been there (see Figure 4).

Indeed, the copy held by the British Library is an example where this 'signature' has carefully been cut away.[9] There are two copies in the Harry Ransom Center, both of them with the Smeeton signature cut away, but one copy has the faint impression of the cut away on the facing page, indicating that it was there for some time before someone removed it, possibly for a sale (see Figure 5).

The *Solimon and Perseda* facsimile seems to have been reasonably popular: there are still copies in a number of libraries, and it is impossible to know how many might be in private hands. Why did Smeeton produce a facsimile of an obscure play like *Solimon and Perseda*? Smeeton did produce other type-facsimiles, but of the many early modern possibilities, this does not seem the most obvious – he did not, for example, produce a facsimile of *The Spanish Tragedy*, which was already in 1805 a play of

---

[9] For a similar strategy which J. Sturt employed on a number of facsimiles of pamphlets printed similarly in Caslon around the period 1810–20, see A. T. Hazen, 'J. Sturt, Facsimilist', *The Library* 25 (1944), 72–9.

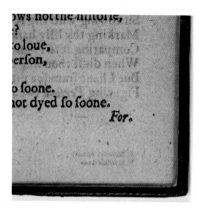

Figure 5 Harry Ransom Center Pforz 953 PFZ

considerable interest. *Solimon and Perseda* was a much more obscure play, though it was available in Thomas Hawkins's three-volume *The Origin of the English Drama*, first published in 1772. Hawkins notes that he based his edition on Garrick's copy of the 1599 edition.[10]

It is possible that the very obscurity of the play facilitated a facsimile designed perhaps to allow people to pretend that they had a copy of a rare edition: the kind of boast some of us might still make about the obscure corners of the early modern world we lay claim to. While copying the ornaments would have taken some time, a type-facsimile was not especially expensive or time-consuming to produce as opposed to a traced facsimile where everything had to be copied meticulously by hand. I cannot determine Smeeton's motives in producing the *Solimon and Perseda* facsimile; I am unsure if he intended to deceive, but deceive he did. Here I beg to differ with Lukas Erne, who is sure that the signature on the verso of the title page means Smeeton intended no deception, but, as I noted earlier, the placement of that signature so close to the bottom edge of the page allows

---

[10] Thomas Hawkins, ed., *The Origins of the English Drama*, 3 vols. (Oxford: Clarendon, 1772), vol. 2, p. 199.

for plausible deniability, so that Smeeton can appeal to two markets: buyers happy with a declared reproduction, and those who might like to pretend that they had an original.[11]

Increasing interest in Kyd during the nineteenth century culminated in what was intended to be an authoritative edition of the play published by Oxford University Press in 1901 and edited by Frederick Boas.[12] Boas followed on from W. W. Greg's mistaken classification of the facsimile as an original copy in Greg's 1900 *List of English Plays*.[13] (Greg lists two British Library copies of the 1599 edition, but one of these, shelfmark G18612, is in fact the Smeeton facsimile.) Accordingly, Boas included the facsimile in his collation of copies of the play and listed variants from it. Meanwhile, Greg had realized his error and, in a rather mean-spirited fashion, reviewed the Boas edition for *The Modern Language Quarterly* and roundly criticized Boas for not realizing that the Smeeton facsimile was not an original text![14] (Boas admitted his mistake in a reissue of the Kyd edition.)

Perhaps the most interesting confusion was manifested in the 1912 Tudor Facsimile Text series edition of the play. This volume is a handsomely produced collotype facsimile, edited by John Farmer, the general editor of the series.[15] Collotype facsimiles used an expensive and labour-intensive photographic process which allows for a much more detailed and fine-grained reproduction of the original. Except in this case, the original was not the original, as Farmer thought, but was in fact the Smeeton facsimile re-facsimiled, so to speak, rearing up again unstoppably like King Charles's Head in Mr Dick's *Memoire* in Dickens's *David Copperfield*. Here, for example, is the telltale final page with the substituted N type in '*FINIS*' (see Figures 6 and 7).

[11] Lukas Erne, ed., *Soliman and Perseda* (Manchester: Manchester University Press, 2014), Malone Society No. 181, pp. viii–ix.

[12] The information which follows is outlined in detail in Hazen, 'Type-Facsimiles', pp. 209–11; see also Erne, *Soliman and Perseda*, pp. viii–ix.

[13] W. W. Greg, *A List of English Plays Written before 1643* (London: Bibliographical Society, 1900), p. 129.

[14] W, W. Greg, review of Boas, *MLQ* 4 (1901): 185–90.

[15] John S. Farmer, ed., *Solimon and Perseda* ('Tudor Facsimile Texts, 1912).

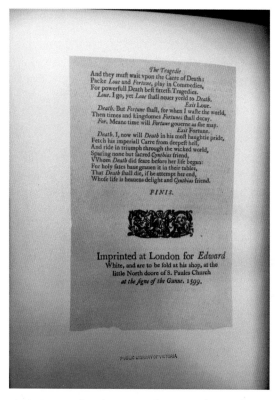

Figure 6 Final page of Tudor Facsimile Texts edition of *Solimon and Perseda*, ed. John Farmer, 1912, State Library of Victoria

A. T. Hazen discussed the ironic further recalibration of the ever-present facsimile in a 1947 article in *Modern Philology*, which was essentially a warning directed at those who had what Hazen termed 'insufficient opportunity' to handle original early modern books.[16]

---

[16] See Hazen, 'Type-Facsimiles', pp. 209–17.

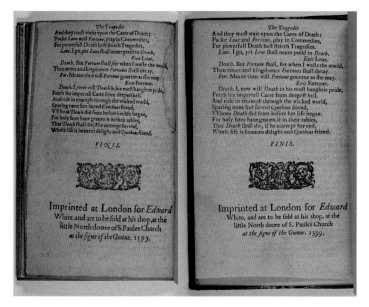

Figure 7 Original final page and Smeeton final page (N in original could not be reproduced in facsimile), Harry Ransom Center, Pforz 953, Pforz 953 PFZ

Hazen was particularly upset that his own library at the University of Chicago had catalogued Smeeton's facsimile as an original volume. This story of the blurring of lines between facsimile and original seems to have reached a redemptive conclusion with the publication in 2014 of Lukas Erne's facsimile edition of the play for the Malone Society. (Founded in 1906, the Malone Society specializes in textual scholarship and has published editions of medieval and early modern texts ever since its foundation.) It goes without saying that Erne is a fine editor, and his introduction, which includes a brief account of the confusion over the Smeeton facsimile, is meticulous. Of course, being a Malone Society edition, the text that Erne prepared is, dare I say it, a facsimile, which seems fitting given the history I have been recounting here. The Malone Society's motto is 'the permanent utility of original texts'. I want to tease this out a bit because it speaks exactly to the paradox I am exploring: the motto means that reproductions of original texts are always useful. The facsimiles stand in place of the original, and over the impressively long history of the Malone Society, their utility (especially for scholars and editors without access to the originals) is not in doubt. However, the ideology behind this idea has of late been under siege: these are patently *not* original texts, but rather highly mediated photographs generally of one specific original copy.

Hazen's plea that scholars must physically handle genuine early modern texts in order to distinguish real from 'fake' has been taken up again by what I am going to call the suspicion of reproduction that has, I think, followed on from the material turn in early modern literary studies. At least to some extent, the story Hazen and I tell does indeed seem like a classic illustration of what happens when lines are blurred between reproduction and original. As I will be discussing in more detail later in this Element, however, the question of why this facsimile might have been produced in the early nineteenth century, and what it tells us about the oscillation between editing and direct access, between material and immaterial texts, relates directly to evolving approaches towards the editing of Shakespeare in particular and early modern drama in general. Prior to the emergence of the photographic facsimile in the mid-nineteenth century, a type-facsimile like Smeeton's offered something to the collector, the curious reader, or the scholar that photography could not: the look and feel of an early modern book. Smeeton used old paper stock, which is another reason he fooled people into thinking they were looking at a 1599 text; but whether this was an act of intentional deception or not, you could say that the type-facsimile of *Soliman and Perseda* aimed to replicate the experience of handling as well as reading an early modern book. This experience, and reproduction in general, have been discussed in some detail in relation to the first folio specifically by Emma Smith.[17] Over the past fifteen years or so, the material turn in early

---

[17] See Emma Smith, *Shakespeare's First Folio: Four Centuries of an Iconic Book* (Oxford: Oxford University Press, 2016), chapter 5.

modern studies that has involved a championing of direct access to early modern book objects has involved, by extension, a turn against these images, with some people starting to sound rather like the society in *Do Androids Dream of Electric Sheep* that sent bounty hunters after replicants, believing they could never come close to original humanity.[18] Again, these issues will be discussed in more detail towards the end of this study, but here I simply want to propose that to understand the place of facsimiles in the textual landscapes of past and present we need to negotiate a middle way that recognizes the affordances as well as drawbacks of facsimiles and reproductions of various kinds.

I am not here to turn away from the new book history that has done so much to vitalize our discipline and has helped my research immeasurably. However, if the tale of the Smeeton facsimile has taught me anything, it is that we cannot default to a simple dichotomy of good original/bad reproduction when it comes to the utility of facsimiles, even if this is a cautionary tale of what sometimes happens when we find ourselves unable to tell the difference between the replicant and the person. Or perhaps, as Smith astutely observes of the first folio facsimile produced by Charlton Hinman from multiple copies of that book at the Folger Shakespeare Library, you can have a facsimile that 'exceeds the original' in its orchestrated perfection.[19] As an Australian who has been doing early modern research for forty-five years, I am also very conscious of the impact textual imaging has had on those of us at the geographic periphery rather than at the centre of the academy. My scholarship would never have happened were it not for the university microfilm series that was the precursor of Early English Books Online. Furthermore, as an editor turning to the digital at the very time when facsimiles/representations are under scrutiny and erasure,

---

[18] For a detailed and prescient analysis of the shortcomings especially of microfilm, see G. Thomas Tanselle, 'Reproductions and Scholarship', *SB* 42 (1989): 25–54; Ian Gadd, 'The Use and Misuse of Early English Books Online', *Literature Compass* 6 (2009): 680–92; and the counter view put succinctly by Zachary Lesser and Whitney Trettien, 'Material/Digital', in Claire M. L. Bourne, ed., *Shakespeare/Text* (London: Bloomsbury, 2021), 402–23.

[19] Smith, *Shakespeare's First Folio*, p. 304.

so to speak, I am trying to juggle my engagement with the necessity of material access in textual studies and the demands of actually accessing the material necessary to do such work. I hold the Smeeton facsimile up as both a warning and a facilitator as this process unfolds. At its heart, my project in this Element is to interrogate easy assumptions about facsimiles and their use, and I hope to equip readers with the knowledge necessary to understand when to embrace and when to question the many different kinds of facsimiles of Shakespeare editions and other early modern books. For now, I'll just end this introduction/story by noting that if you look for *Solimon and Perseda* on Google Books you'll get images of (yes, you guessed it!) not the original, but the Smeeton facsimile!

1 The Prehistory of Facsimiles: Eighteenth-Century Editing

Before the advent of print, copying by hand was the means whereby texts were transmitted, and this process of manuscript transmission anticipates in many ways the interrelationship between printed texts and facsimiles. The expectation that a scribe is copying a manuscript accurately comes up against the human factors leading to inevitable variation, whether accidental or deliberate. The advent of print offered what we might call the illusion of the perfect and exact reproduction of texts, though we now know that for early modern printed books almost every copy was unique because of the process of continuous press correction (where errors were fixed during the print run), and through minute variations in the wear on type, patterns of binding, and pagination. The idea of a facsimile makes most sense in the context of a printing process (such as photography) that invites duplication, as opposed to the common early modern process whereby each successive edition of a text changed by using the preceding printed edition as a base upon which changes (both deliberate and unintended) were wrought. This earlier process is especially evident in the succeeding editions of the Shakespeare folio, where, as Sonia Massai has explained, each new edition built upon and could be said to be an edition of its most immediate predecessor.[20]

---

[20] Sonia Massai, *Shakespeare and the Rise of the Editor* (Cambridge: Cambridge University Press, 2007).

The 1623 folio edition of thirty-six Shakespeare plays was published seven years after the playwright's death. The complete title of the volume is *Mr. William Shakespeares Comedies, Histories, & Tragedies. Published according to the True Originall Copies*. As my analysis of facsimiles suggests, the idea of 'true original copies' contains a number of ambiguities. A 'copy' might be either a source, or a reproduction of that source, and it is this paradox which, as I have already noted, reverberates throughout the history of facsimiles. As Smith observes, the claim made on the folio title page 'mobilizes a number of concepts about authenticity and reproducibility that echo through [the folio's] subsequent history'.[21] The 'original' of a Shakespeare play recedes into the distance the more we try to recreate it, as various editorial theories that try to reconstruct the source of the printed texts find to their cost. The 'original' copies of these plays exist only in the form of their aftermath.

As salesmen, John Heminge and Henry Condell (Shakespeare's actor colleagues who helped assemble the playtexts for printing in the first folio) needed to maintain that their copies of the original copies were more authentic and reliable than copies that had come before. As they claim in their preface 'to the great Variety of Readers': 'as where (before) you were abus'd with diuerse stolne, and surreptitious copies, maimed, and deformed by the frauds and stealthes of iniurious impostors, that expos'd them: euen those, are now offer'd to your view cur'd, and perfect of their limbes; and all the rest, absolute in their numbers, as he conceiued them' (sig. A3r). Here a (false) dichotomy is set up between copies that are defective and the copy (of a copy) that is guaranteed to be perfect. Yet this oscillation, as I will argue at greater length later in this Element, exemplifies the way that beneath the facsimile, or the copy, is not really solid ground, but a further copy, because all reproduction involves variation/mediation.

An even closer ally (aesthetically speaking) to the facsimile of a printed text is forgery, where we find a long history of entanglement between original and 'imitation': is it a copy or a fake? In his groundbreaking work on this topic, Anthony Grafton traces the burgeoning of forgeries back to the fourth century BCE, which he describes as the 'first real heyday of the

---

[21] Smith, *Shakespeare's First Folio*, p. 280.

forger and the critic'.[22] Grafton argues that there is a symbiotic relationship between forgery and scholarly critique, where the intersection is historicism. In other words, there can be no forgery without an understanding of the historical specificity of texts, and there can be no detection of forgery without a concomitant knowledge of how a text is located in time. In the same way, in order to have any currency, a facsimile requires of its maker an understanding of historical context for a text, and a knowledge of how texts were made, however rudimentary that understanding might be. So, in recounting the history of facsimiles of printed texts, I want to underline the fact that the groundwork for these facsimiles was a sense of the value of the 'original' text, rather than an unthinking acceptance of adaptations, editions, and modernizations of those texts as adequate surrogates.

From this perspective, I will rehearse briefly the way that Shakespeare was edited in the eighteenth century. It is a sequence of events that can be seen as paving the way for the growth in interest in facsimiles. While I focus on Shakespeare, the developments I describe also relate to other early modern texts, especially plays, as well as a selection of medieval works. Recent bibliographical work has emphasized the surge in status for Shakespeare late in the seventeenth century, not only with the publication of the fourth folio in 1685, but also with some sheets printed around 1700 in a version that has been nominated as a fifth folio.[23] This period should be understood as a tipping point, because this folio was the last of its format: collections of Shakespeare's works would shift from what we might call a palimpsest to an edition. By this I mean that the successive folios build upon each other, but do not start afresh each time (except in so far as the third folio added seven new plays). Rather, each adapted its immediate

---

[22] Anthony Grafton, *Forgers and Critics: Creativity and Duplicity in Western Scholarship*, new edition (Princeton, NJ: Princeton University Press, 2019), p. 24.

[23] See Lara Hanson and Eric Rasmussen, 'Shakespeare without Rules: The Fifth Shakespeare Folio and Market Demand in the Early 1700s', in Emma Depledge and Peter Kirwan, eds., *Canonising Shakespeare: Stationers and the Book Trade 1640–1740* (Cambridge: Cambridge University Press, 2017), pp. 55–62; Emma Depledge, *Shakespeare's Rise to Cultural Prominence: Politics, Print and Alteration* (Cambridge: Cambridge University Press, 2018).

predecessor. This includes the book format, which remained recognizably the same size and layout through the four folio editions of 1623, 1632, 1663/ 4, and 1685. The only notable change in the fourth folio was a structural one, with standardized pagination (rather than pagination starting again at the beginning of each genre section). Even though it is now possible, following on from Sonia Massai's influential study of unnamed editorial work, to see localized textual changes in the successive folios as evidence of a process we might call proto-editing, they are still clearly part of a continuity in the publication of Shakespeare's plays as a collection, a process that can also be compared to the two Beaumont and Fletcher folios of 1647 and 1679.[24] (It is important to note the quite different trajectory of Shakespeare's poetry, where the publisher John Benson's 1640 edition of the poetry dramatically rearranged the sonnets, changed pronouns to shift the addressee of numbers of sonnets from male to female, often recast the short lyrics as longer poems, and integrated a number of poems clearly not by Shakespeare.[25])

The shift from the palimpsest to the more recognizable edition has been traced in Andrew Murphy's comprehensive account of the print publication of Shakespeare.[26] As well as the four seventeenth-century folios, individual Shakespeare plays in quarto format (single-title pamphlets roughly the size of a modern paperback) continued to be published routinely over the course of the century. Murphy notes that, in contrast to the folios, quarto editions of individual plays remained

---

[24] By this I simply mean that the complex canon of Beaumont and Fletcher – complex both bibliographically and textually – was packaged in the folio, collected format similarly to Shakespeare's and indeed to Ben Jonson's.

[25] *Poems: Written by Wil. Shake-Speare. Gent* (1640); see the pioneering study by Sasha Roberts, *Reading Shakespeare's Poems in Early Modern England* (Basingstoke: Palgrave Macmillan, 2002); Megan Heffernan, 'Turning Sonnets into Poems: Textual Affect and John Benson's Metaphysical Shakespeare', *Shakespeare Quarterly* 64 (2013): 71–98; and the excellent recent study by Jane Kingsley-Smith, *The Afterlife of Shakespeare's Sonnets* (Cambridge: Cambridge University Press, 2019), chapter 2.

[26] Andrew Murphy, *Shakespeare in Print*, second edition (Cambridge: Cambridge University Press, 2021).

popular through the eighteenth century, especially in the form of versions which were acted, and were accordingly closer to adaptations than to versions of original quartos.[27] From this perspective, the first publication that leaves quarto and folio reprintings behind, and looks more like a 'modern' edition, was financed by the publisher Jacob Tonson in 1709, and edited by the playwright Nicholas Rowe.[28] The eighteenth-century editions of Shakespeare have been the subject of considerable scholarly attention, and here I intend only to outline the way that they were the necessary precondition that led to the parallel production of facsimiles later in the century. In many respects, the 1709 Rowe edition exemplifies the shift from the seventeenth-century folios and quartos to eighteenth-century editions. There are, though, a number of interesting continuities with the seventeenth-century folios: there are no notes of any kind in either the folios or the 1709 edition, and while Rowe tells us he has compared 'the several editions', he does not provide any information about this apparent collation process. The 1709 edition is elegant, however, with a crisp typeface and well-set-out pages in a set of easy-to-handle octavo volumes (slightly smaller than quarto size). Publication in six volumes also ensured ease of use: while the folios would have to be set up on a reading lectern or desk, the Rowe edition (and its successors) could easily be held in the hand and carried or read pretty well anywhere. (When nicely bound, they also looked good on the owner's bookshelves.) As Peter Holland notes in his detailed discussion of Rowe's approach to *The Tempest*, '[I]t is Rowe whose work transforms

---

[27] For an original account of how publishers and printers constructed printed plays so as to reflect their status as records of performance through to the eighteenth century, see Claire M. L. Bourne, *Typographies of Performance in Early Modern England* (Oxford: Oxford University Press, 2020).

[28] For a clever reimagining of the fourth folio as an outmoded book, especially for an enthusiastic Restoration theatregoer, see Don-John Dugas, *Marketing the Bard: Shakespeare in Performance and Print 1660–1740* (Columbia: University of Missouri Press, 2006), p. 71, and his detailed discussion of the marketing of Shakespeare through the early eighteenth-century editions in sections 2–4.

the appearance of Shakespeare's printed language into a form we can still comfortably recognize as modern.'[29] For the next edition in 1714, the format shifted from octavo to duodecimo (about 15 per cent smaller), making the volumes even more portable without losing much clarity, and as Mathieu Bouchard has shown recently, the edition was revised quite extensively, probably by John Hughes.[30]

As many scholars of the eighteenth-century editions have pointed out, the next complete works edition, published in 1725, saw Alexander Pope alter and emend the text to match more exactly eighteenth-century standards of good writing.[31] My point here, again, is not to rehearse the easy criticisms of this move (although Pope's edition has been rehabilitated of late), but rather to note how Pope's approach moved the text further away from the earliest editions, not simply in terms of modernized spelling and punctuation, but also in word choice, reaching down to phrases and even entire speeches and scenes.[32] The other major shift in the eighteenth century is that Tonson's elegant editions encouraged other publishers to compete, either with imitations, such as the purported seventh volume of the Rowe edition containing the poetry (which was, in fact, a creation of Edmund Curll and Egbert Sanger), or with more affordable editions of the plays.[33]

---

[29] Peter Holland, 'Modernizing Shakespeare: Nicholas Rowe and *The Tempest*', *Shakespeare Quarterly* 51 (2000): 24.

[30] Mathieu D. S. Bouchard, 'A Revised Account of the 1714 *Works of Mr. William Shakespear*', *Papers of the Bibliographical Society of America* 115 (2021): 419–61; see Murphy, *Shakespeare in Print*, p. 91.

[31] *The Works of Shakespeare in Six Volumes, Collated and Corrected by* [sic] *the former editions, by Mr Pope* (1725); and see, for example, Jonathan H. Holmes, 'Alexander Pope, Interventionist Editing and *The Taming of the Shew* (1725)', in *Canonising Shakespeare*, pp. 187–200.

[32] See Simon Jarvis, *Scholars and Gentlemen: Shakespearean Textual Criticism and Representations of Scholarly Labour, 1725–1765* (Oxford: Clarendon, 1995), pp. 51–62.

[33] See, for example, Aleida Auld, 'Canon/Apocrypha', in *Shakespeare/Text*, pp. 102–20, and Holger Schott Syme, 'Book/Theatre, also in *Shakespeare/ Text*, pp. 223–44.

The most significant development, for my purposes, however, was the edition Lewis Theobald prepared as a kind of counter to Pope. It is not the dispute with Pope that makes this a key moment, but rather the way that Theobald approached the page layout of his edition. Before moving to those specifics of Theobald's edition, it is necessary first to summarize his clash with Pope, given that it has had the unfortunate effect of making Theobald more a figure of fun than a key player in the progress of editorial methodology. Theobald provoked Pope by writing an extensive critique of Pope's edition, published in 1726, entitled *Shakespeare Restor'd or, A Specimen of the Many Errors as well Committed, or Unamended, by Mr Pope*. In the first edition of *The Dunciad*, published in 1728, Pope took what was to be a lengthy revenge against Theobald, depicting him as the favourite of Dulness:

> Here studious I unlucky Moderns save,
> Nor sleeps one error in its father's grave,
> Old puns restore, lost blunders nicely seek,
> And crucify poor *Shakespear* once a week.[34]

In the end, Tonson contracted Theobald to produce an edition that would supersede Pope's. Theobald produced an emended edition, although recent scholars have pointed out that this was in fact achieved through revising Pope's text, rather than starting completely afresh.[35] However, as noted previously, a key change introduced by Theobald was a running series of footnotes explaining aspects of the text, as well as offering commentary (however inconsistent) on textual sources, cruxes, and emendations. Accordingly, for the first time, this edition of Shakespeare looks quite similar to the modern kind of edition with which we are all familiar. Here is a typical page, which can readily be compared to the equivalent page of the first folio (see Figures 8 and 9).

Theobald's note (number 10) is what we might call a typical editorial explanation for an emendation. It initiates the tradition of historicizing

---

[34] Alexander Pope, *The Dunciad* (1728), Bk. 1.

[35] For a succinct summary, see Murphy, *Shakespeare in Print*, pp. 101–4.

Figure 8 Lewis Theobald, ed., *The Works of Shakespeare* (1733), pp. 18–19,
State Library of Victoria

emendations: the change of assignation of the speech from Miranda to
Prospero (which Theobald takes up) was first put in place by Dryden.
We are also offered a theatrical explanation for this change. Most of all, we
can see clearly how far we have come from the unadorned folio page. It is
true that alterations of punctuation, for example, are unmarked, but I would
argue that this is the moment when an aesthetic and conceptual distance
starts to open up between the original text, and the later edition. As Andrew
Murphy notes, '[T]he general principles of [Theobald's] textual programme
were ... foundational for much of what followed in Shakespeare editing.'[36]

[36] Ibid., p. 104.

Figure 9 Shakespeare first folio, Brandeis University Copy

In the second half of the eighteenth century, this process continued in a variety of ways. For example, Edward Capell's reputation and recognition for his originality as an editor have steadily grown from his initial characterization as eccentric and isolated.[37] Capell's edition was published in 1767–8, but his extensive notes were published separately in stages between 1774 and 1783. However much this was the product of poor organization, it had the effect of anticipating another influential form of edition still in evidence today, where only some textual notes are placed on the page while longer annotations are placed either at the end of the volume or, in Capell's case, in separate volumes. So here are examples of Capell's treatment of *The Tempest* (see Figures 10 and 11).

This discussion is not intended to be an exhaustive account of eighteenth-century editions, but I will conclude with the editor who, as Margreta de Grazia has argued, did the most to consolidate a certain notion of Shakespeare as an authorial presence that is brought into being through a particular editorial process: Edmond Malone.[38] In her subtle and complex argument, de Grazia associates Malone's edition with a radical shift in the idea of a consolidated authorial presence as a paradigm for a concomitant shift in notions of individuality. As de Grazia sums up this shift: Malone 'prepared the text for readers by disciplining it and it has prepared readers for the text by instructing them'.[39] In his preface to his 1790 edition, Malone underlines the fact that his editorial methodology involved 'a careful collation of the oldest copies'.[40] As de Grazia again notes, 'The new criterion of authenticity converted the Shakespearean texts into a new kind of object: one lodged in the past rather than integral to current cultural concerns.'[41] Malone's notes also shift towards a comprehensive recapitulation of the view of earlier editors, with his page looking even more like

---

[37] See, for example, the discussion of Capell's innovative approach to referencing in Alan Galey and Rebecca Niles, 'Moving Parts: Digital Modeling and the Infrastructures of Shakespeare Editing', *Shakespeare Quarterly* 68 (2017): pp. 44–9.

[38] Margreta de Grazia, *Shakespeare Verbatim: The Reproduction of Authenticity and the 1790 Apparatus* (Oxford: Clarendon, 1991).

[39] Ibid., p. 226.

[40] Edmond Malone, ed., *The Plays and Poems of Shakespeare* (1890), vol. 1, p. v.

[41] De Grazia, *Shakespeare Verbatim*, p. 71.

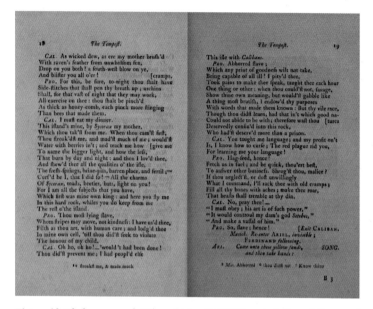

Figure 10 *Shakespeare*, ed. Edward Capell (1768), vol. 1. State Library of Victoria

a modern single play scholarly edition, where notes tend to dominate the text (Figure 12).

Malone consolidated a movement towards historicism that marked the progression of eighteenth-century editing, although, again as de Grazia notes, it is important not to fall into a teleological misconception that the editions mark an unwavering 'progress'.[42] Both in terms of book format and in terms of page layout and information design, the sequence of eighteenth-century editions discussed here illustrates an increasing

[42] On this point see also the careful discussion in Marcus Walsh, *Shakespeare, Milton and Eighteenth-Century Literary Editing: The Beginnings of Interpretative Scholarship* (Cambridge: Cambridge University Press, 1997), p. 23 and passim.

line the firſt, is ſingl'd out by one editor as a term that comes under the ſaid remark concerning Caliban's language: but it's ſenſe is—miſchievous, ſerving miſchievous purposes; and it may be us'd in that ſenſe by any character, even at this day: Had he ſingl'd out "*vaſt, vaſt of night,*" (l. 7.) for explanation only, there might be those who had thank'd him; for certainly 'tis both a rare and a hard one, nor ſhould the *Gloſſary* have overpaſſ'd it: it's ſenſe approaches to—waſte, and we apprehend by it an idea of "*night*" as a waſte part of time.

19. 2.

Pro. Abhorred ſlave; &c.] Firſt adjudg'd to the ſpeaker it now comes from, by Mr. Dryden the play's alterer into one intitl'd by him —"*The enchanted Iſland;*" and firſt taken into Shakeſpeare's editions by their third modern publiſher: the adopter is almoſt diffuſe in his reasons for it, but they present themſelves readily; what he ſays of the change's cauſe may be right,—that it ſprang of players' not liking that a character of Miranda's importance ſhould ſtand ſo long on the ſtage without a ſhare of the dialogue. ∽ The changes in 6 & 7. were (it ſeems) propos'd to the publick in a work of the fifth modern's that was prior to his predeceſſor's edition, who has given them place in it: their fitneſs (indeed neceſſity, as ſeems to this editor)

lyes in this;—that the whole animal world, each individual of it, cannot but have *knowledge* of what itſelf *purposes;* and to a large part of it is given means of expreſſing those purposes, by look, action, or ſound: Caliban, as a brute, had his purposes, and ſome means of expreſſing them; but ſhort of what his human part might have, and of what it had at this time through Proſpero's teaching; and it is with this benefit's evil reception that he is reproach'd in that paſſage, as his anſwer evinces. The epithet given "*plague*" in that anſwer is characteriſtic of the diſtemper in a more eminent manner than belongs to other eruptions. "*Setebas,*" in 26, is from Hakluit.

D'. 31.

Come unto these yellow ſands, &c.] The whole of this wild ſong is printed with great negligence in copies preceding the ſecond modern's: his tranſpoſal in 20, 4, and the parenthetical poſition of the ſecond line over it by the fifth modern, have clear'd up the firſt part; but the laſt they have paſſ'd over; and yet certainly, as it has ſtood 'till this present, it could give no idea of the manner it was perform'd in: There is direction for a "*burthen,*" or chorus, but no words aſſign'd for it: it came in therefore at the words—"*Hark, hark;*" and conſiſted of a muſick that ſeem'd to come from all parts of the ſtage,

Figure 11 Edward Capell, *Notes and Various Readings to Shakespeare* (1783), vol. 2, p. 60. State Library of Victoria

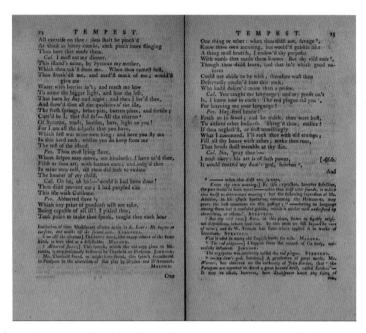

Figure 12 Edmond Malone, ed., *The Plays and Poems of William Shakespeare* (1790), vol. 1 part 2. State Library of Victoria

physical and aesthetic distance from the original texts. This visual shift was combined with an increasing editorial interest in moving back to the earliest editions, rather than just emending a more recent edition, which was often the most recent edition available. Accordingly, the bulk of these eighteenth-century editions of Shakespeare revalued the earliest texts, while at the same time producing volumes that were less and less like them. This investment in textual history was complicated by the increasing scarcity of those original texts, which were being bought by collectors and antiquarians (and indeed editors), and which also succumbed to wear and tear.

This simultaneous move away from the earliest texts, and revaluing them as 'authentic' sources, did not apply only to Shakespeare; four further notable examples are the dramatic works of Jonson and of Beaumont and Fletcher, and the poetry of Spenser and of Milton. Tonson published the works of Beaumont and Fletcher in seven volumes in 1711. Again, as was the case with Shakespeare, we see a shift from the folio publication of this collection in 1647 and 1679 to the multivolume, 'corrected', and illustrated eighteenth-century edition. This edition had no notes of any kind, but this was remedied in the 1750 edition, which featured notes by Theobald (augmented after his death). This editorial process culminated in the 1778 edition, which has some parallels with the 1778 Steevens Shakespeare edition, and which, as Ivan Lupić and Brett Greatley-Hirsch noted in a fascinating article, attracted the attention of Malone, who annotated his copy with mostly editorial interventions.[43]

A similar situation pertained for Jonson. A six-volume illustrated edition of Jonson, largely based on the 1692 folio of his works, was published in 1715–16. Then a collated and annotated edition was published in seven volumes in 1756, edited by Peter Whalley. Spenser and Milton have more complex eighteenth-century histories, but, for my purposes here, eighteenth-century editions of their works produce the same effect of increasing distance from the physical appearance of primary texts, combined with a new attention paid to those texts as editorial sources. The complex details of Spenser's reception in the eighteenth century, and the five substantial editions published between 1715 and 1795, can be traced in detail through Hazel Wilkinson's careful study *Edmund Spenser and the Eighteenth-Century Book*.[44] The publication of Spenser editions once again begins in the early eighteenth century with a six-volume Tonson edition in 1715. Thomas Birch edited *The Faerie*

---

[43] Ivan Lupić and Brett Greatley-Hirsch, '"What Stuff Is Here?" Edmond Malone and the 1778 Edition of Beaumont and Fletcher', *Papers of the Bibliographical Society of America* 111 (2017): 287–315.

[44] Hazel Wilkinson, *Edmund Spenser and the Eighteenth-Century Book* (Cambridge: Cambridge University Press, 2017).

Queene in three volumes in 1751 in an edition that contained notable illustrations by William Kent and a glossary. The first two annotated editions of *The Faerie Queene* were published in 1759: the Tonson volumes edited by John Upton, and an edition by Ralph Church published by William Faden.[45] Upton provided a huge array of annotations, placed apart from the text in a second volume, while Church paid close attention to the earliest texts, favouring the first quartos, at least as far as Spenser's spelling was concerned.

Finally, there is Milton, who attracted editors shortly after the first publication of *Paradise Lost* in 1667. Tonson published a handsome, illustrated folio edition in 1688, taking the poem (visually) a considerable distance from its first appearance.[46] Tonson then published several editions of different shapes and sizes, until the controversial edition undertaken by the classical scholar Richard Bentley, which was published in 1732. Bentley produced a heavily emended edition, rather like Theobald on steroids, and, in so doing, attracted the same kind of ire from Pope. However, a sober and scholarly corrective appeared with Thomas Newton's edition of 1749, which was reprinted nine times up to 1790.[47] Once again, this edition moves a considerable distance from the physical appearance of the original text and indeed looks very similar to a heavily annotated, scholarly, modern edition, with many pages featuring only a single line of text, with the rest of the page taken up by two columns of annotation (see Figure 13).[48]

These accumulating eighteenth-century editions paved the way for the popularity of facsimiles, given that originals were not only more valued – and scarcer – but also far less able to be pictured or imagined through the lens of new editions, given the transformation of *mise-en-page*. In response to the earliest (and most authoritative) editions growing scarcer and more

---

[45] See ibid., chapter 4.

[46] See R. G. Moyles, *The Text of Paradise Lost* (Toronto: University of Toronto Press, 1985).

[47] Ibid., p. 76, and see the detailed account in Walsh, *Shakespeare, Milton and Eighteenth-Century Literary Editing*, chapter 3.

[48] In this sense, the eighteenth-century editions of English literature hark back to seventeenth-century editions of classical writing which were heavily annotated.

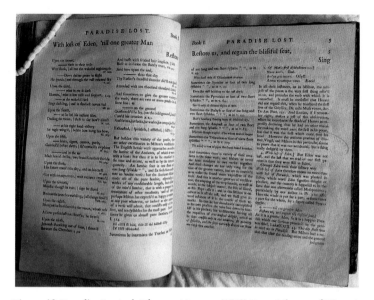

Figure 13 *Paradise Lost*, ed. Thomas Newton (1749) State Library of Victoria

valued from a scholarly and antiquarian perspective, yet also less easily pictured in light of developments in editorial page design, facsimiles became increasingly popular from the very end of the eighteenth century as stand-ins for harder-to-access originals.

Two significant precursors to the full facsimiles are worth considering. The first is an edition of Shakespeare quartos edited by George Steevens and published in four volumes in 1766. Steevens went on to produce a full edition of Shakespeare's works (with slight assistance from Samuel Johnson) in 1773, but the edition of the quartos, while not exactly a set of facsimiles, went to some length to reproduce the appearance of the pages of the original volumes. Steevens undertook a collation of the early quartos when, to the best of his knowledge, they survived in variant states and editions. The evocation of the appearance of the original texts is best illustrated by his treatment of the sonnets, where, for example, the dedication page is a close (albeit not exact) copy of the original (see Figures 14A and 14B).

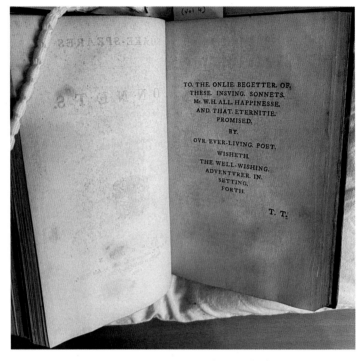

Figure 14A George Steevens, ed., *Twenty of the Plays of Shakespeare* (1766), vol. 3 Figure 14B 1609 page, Folger Shakespeare Library

The play quartos are less like type-facsimiles, but they too evoke the originals, if not entirely replicate them (Figure 15).

My second example is a more self-conscious attempt to recreate the appearance of an early edition. Capell Lofft was the nephew of Shakespeare editor Edward Capell and something of an autodidact. In 1792, he published an edition of the first book of *Paradise Lost*, followed

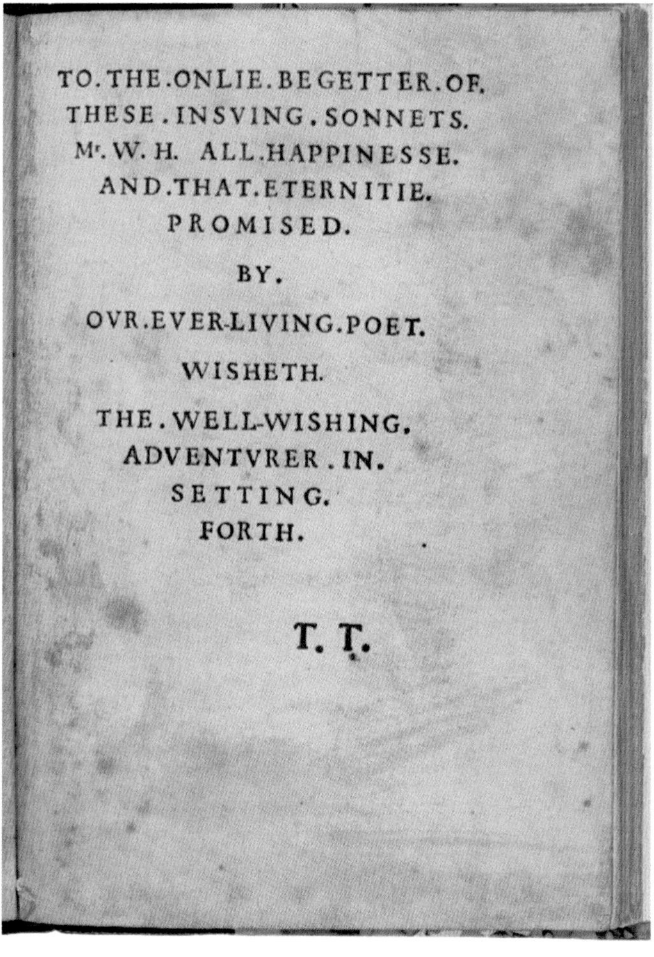

TO. THE. ONLIE. BEGETTER. OF.
THESE . INSVING . SONNETS.
M^r. W. H.   ALL .HAPPINESSE.
AND. THAT. ETERNITIE.
PROMISED.

BY.

OVR. EVER-LIVING. POET.

WISHETH.

THE . WELL-WISHING.
ADVENTVRER . IN.
SETTING.
FORTH.

T. T.

Figure 14B

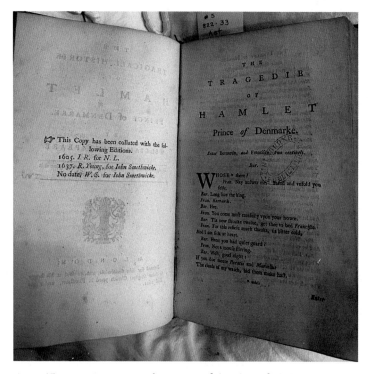

Figure 15 George Steevens, ed., *Twenty of the Plays of Shakespeare* (1766), *Hamlet*, vol. 4. State Library of Victoria

by a second edition in 1793, which contained the first and second books. (Lofft never published the rest of the poem.) Lofft wrote a lengthy preface containing a careful consideration of the early editions and a declaration that 'The design of this Edition is to give the PARADISE LOST correctly, and in such manner as MILTON intended.'[49] Lofft was very conscious of matching at least some aspects of the physical appearance of the first, ten-book edition of *Paradise Lost*

---

[49] Capel Lofft, ed., *Paradise Lost* (1792), sig. a.

(published in 1667): 'The size of the page of the first Edition is very near equal to the present; the type similar, though a little smaller.'[50] However, in a fascinating editorial move, Lofft decided that the original punctuation impeded an understanding of Milton's verse, and so Lofft invented a form of pointing to aid the reader in understanding the rhythm of the poem; this has the effect of countering the imitation of the original's layout and typography, with an at times eccentric recasting of the punctuation (see Figure 16).

Lofft's somewhat quixotic 'correction' of modern editions of *Paradise Lost*, which involved an attempted return to the physical appearance of the original, albeit with the addition of his highly individual punctuation to assist verse pronunciation, is a precursor to the emergence of fully fledged facsimiles of the kind exemplified by *Solimon and Perseda*.

As I have been arguing, the rise in quantity and quality of editions of Shakespeare and other early modern writers during the course of the eighteenth century paved the way for type-facsimiles. This is because the editions became further removed from the physical appearance of the original texts, while at the same time, the textually sensitive approach of editors made more people aware of how significant the early editions were. Finally, there was a gradual rise in what we might call an antiquarian interest in, and at times obsession with, collecting old and often rare volumes, and where these were not readily available, or were imperfect, facsimiles stepped in to make up the gap. The dramatic increase in the numbers of almost obsessive collectors of old volumes in the nineteenth century increased the competition for both original books and methods of supplementing them or repairing/perfecting them. Where twentieth-century individual collectors and, increasingly, rare book libraries were suspicious of 'inauthentic' volumes, or volumes that showed evidence of insertions of facsimile pages, nineteenth-century collectors, as I will explain in more detail later in this Element, had a more lenient view of the concept of authenticity. Paradoxically, the quest for the authentic went along with increasingly sophisticated methods of reproduction and of book history that questioned the very notion of the authentic, 'original' early modern book.

---

[50] Ibid., sig. a2.

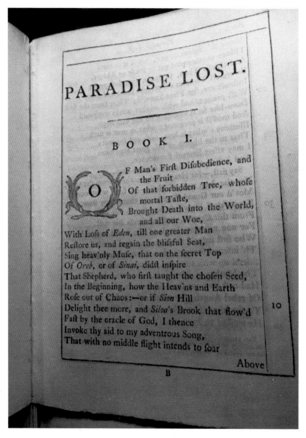

Figure 16 Capel Lofft, ed., *Paradise Lost* (1792), Newberry Library

2 Searching for Reproduction: Traced and Type-Facsimiles

The first ambitious type-facsimile intended to reach a relatively wide audience, not surprisingly, was of Shakespeare's first folio. Although I say 'not surprisingly', a type-facsimile of a book as large as the first folio was a considerable undertaking on a scale many times larger than producing a single play quarto like *Solimon and Perseda*. The production of such a facsimile again underlines the point I have been making about the increasing interest in the nature of original texts, especially as the canonization of Shakespeare was reaching a peak at the beginning of the nineteenth century.[51] In 1807, E. and J. Wright published their first folio facsimile; their identity as publishers is clearly visible on the verso of the title page, which itself pastes in a reproduction of the Droeshout portrait and is a convincing reproduction of the most iconic of all title pages (see Figures 17, 18, and 19).[52]

However, this attempt at faithfulness does not extend to the rest of the facsimile, where, one can only assume, cost savings mean that ornamentation is set aside in favour of a much plainer appearance than the original. A good example is the first page of *The Tempest*, where we lose the ornamental headpiece and the ornamental capital (see Figures 20 and 21).

Of course, this deficiency would only be apparent to someone who had a first folio, or who had access to one, as a point of comparison. As we can see by comparing the pages, the lineation, spelling, italicization, two-column layout, and so on are all replicated with commendable accuracy, even if the ornaments are missing. Again, I would stress that the very appeal of this facsimile is bound up with the combination of an increasing desire to own something like the original and the increasingly limited possibilities of accessing an original text. One can see this first folio facsimile as recapitulating both the drawbacks and the benefits of a type-facsimile like *Soliman and Perseda*: this facsimile certainly offers a sense of what the folio was like, although unfortunately, as I will discuss shortly, it contained numerous individual errors. Still, a key benefit of owning such a book was that it offered a 'complete'

---

[51] On Shakespeare as icon, see, for example, Charles LaPorte, *The Victorian Cult of Shakespeare* (Cambridge: Cambridge University Press, 2020).

[52] For a brief account of both the Wright facsimile and the succeeding Booth facsimile, see Smith, *Shakespeare's First Folio*, pp. 306–9; I can find no information on the impressive reproduction of the Droeshout engraving.

Figure 17 E. and J. Wright facsimile of first folio, 1807, Newberry Library

Shakespeare in one volume at a time when all the current editions were in multiple volumes. It took another generation before the idea that a household might have at minimum two books, the Bible and Shakespeare, was taken up by editors and the book trade, when the

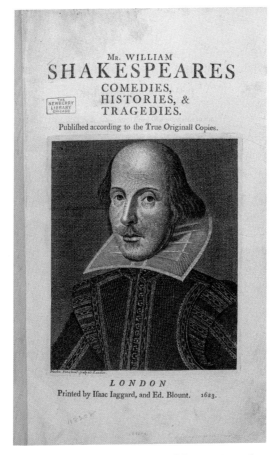

Figure 18 E. and J. Wright facsimile of first folio, 1807, Newberry Library

first popular, cheap, and accessible one-volume Shakespeare was edited by Charles Knight and published in 1845. As outlined previously in this section, by 1807, readers had access to a variety of multivolume editions produced during the course of the eighteenth century, but there were no

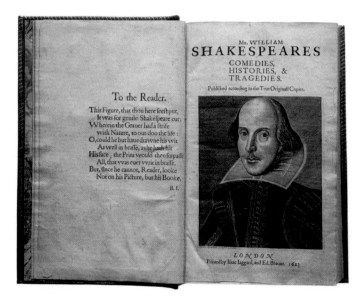

Figure 19 First folio title page, Folger Shakespeare Library

single-volume editions available, and none became available until 1845.[53] Neither was there any attempt at another type-facsimile of the folio until Lionel Booth produced one in 1863–4. This new facsimile of the first folio did follow on from a rather belated assessment of the accuracy of the Wright facsimile in *Notes and Queries* in 1853. There it

---

[53] See Murphy, *Shakespeare in Print*, Appendix. Murphy notes a two-volume edition by William Miller in 1806. Later in the century, in 1864, the one-volume Globe Shakespeare was to have a far-reaching impact both upon its publication and through successive editions, and then, as we will see, it was reincarnated as the basis of a popular online edition. See Margreta de Grazia, 'The Question of the One and the Many: The Globe Shakespeare, the *Complete King Lear*, and the New Folger Library Shakespeare', *Shakespeare Quarterly* 46 (1995): 245–51.

Figure 20 E. and J. Wright facsimile of first folio, 1807, Newberry Library

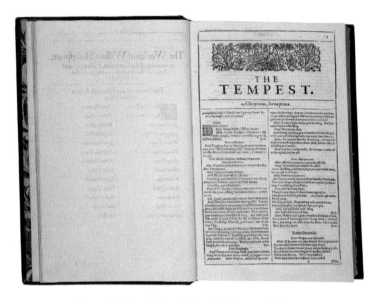

Figure 21 First folio, Folger Shakespeare Library

was reported that the book collector William Upcott had collated the Wright facsimile and found '368 typographical errors' – although it should be noted that this is not a great percentage given the size of the folio.[54] There is no information about which original copy Upcott used for this collation, and the number and nature of errors would depend upon how 'corrected' the original copy was. Indeed, this underlines the fact that facsimiles of early modern books reproduce a single original, and there are always variations between each individual copy owing to press correction and other contingencies related to moveable type printing.

[54] 'The reprint, in 1808 [*sic*], of the first folio edition of Shakespeare', *N&Q* (8 January 1853).

Some significant quarto facsimiles were published between the Wright first folio facsimile and the Booth first folio facsimile (published between 1863 and 1864). I will discuss these quarto facsimiles shortly, but at this point it is worth discussing the Booth facsimile as it represents a kind of monument to the type-facsimile process just before the advent of photographic facsimiles, which largely made the type-facsimile redundant. Lionel Booth's type-facsimile was published in three parts (*Comedies*, 1863, *Histories*, 1863 and *Tragedies*, 1864), but the parts were intended to be bound together into a single volume, for which the 1864 publication provided a separate title page: *Shakespeare As Put Forth in 1623*. Booth had the clever idea of replicating pagination and layout but reducing the size of the type and pages, resulting in a more compact book as well as one that was a far better replica than the Wright example, which also contained the ornamental features of the original.[55] It is evident even from the image I include here that Booth's facsimile is eminently readable, despite its shrunken format, given that it has the advantage over many a one-volume Shakespeare of being easy to hold and quite portable (Figure 22).

Prior to the publication of Charlton Hinman's first folio facsimile of 1968 (discussed in Section 5), A number of scholars saw Booth's facsimile as the most significant Shakespeare facsimile and, despite being a type-facsimile, the most reliable. This touches on an issue to which I will return: while people may initially have been seduced by the idea that the photographic facsimile had to be the most accurate, photographic facsimiles actually had many flaws and could, in a sense, be trumped by type-facsimiles done with sufficient care, especially as far as the legibility of individual letters and at times whole words was concerned. Indeed, some of the later positive assessments of the Booth facsimile stem from scholars who were enthusiasts for type-facsimiles (over photographic facsimiles), or who were at least prepared to weigh up the pros and cons of the various types of facsimile that were available. In an influential article on facsimiles published in *The Library* in 1926, the bibliographer A. W. Pollard

---

[55] Booth did produce a small number of full-sized copies for the luxury market, but the bulk of the printing was in the reduced size format.

Figure 22 Lionel Booth, *Shakespeare As Put Forth in 1623* (1864), State Library of Victoria

carefully considered the advantages and disadvantages of each kind of facsimile. Of the Booth facsimile, he declared: 'This is still a very useful book because of its handy size and clear type and its extraordinary accuracy.'[56] It is in this pioneering set of articles, originally presented as talks to the Bibliographical Society, that W. W. Greg (an even more influential bibliographer and textual editor than Pollard) came up with the apt aphorism: '[P]hotographic reproductions are reliable but illegible, reprints are legible but unreliable.'[57]

Before turning to the theoretical issues surrounding photographic facsimiles, I need to return to an earlier period in the nineteenth century and to a series of facsimiles of Shakespeare quartos. The most notable of these was a type-facsimile of a newly discovered copy of the formerly lost first edition of Shakespeare's most famous play: *Hamlet*. The whole story of the discovery of the previously unknown first quarto of *Hamlet*, and the effect of its resurfacing on everything from conceptions of authorship and editing, through to interpretations of the play and its complex afterlives, has been analysed recently in a remarkable book by Zachary Lesser: *Hamlet after Q1*.[58] After the discovery of an imperfect copy of this quarto in the closet of a country house in 1823, arrangements were swiftly made to publish a type-facsimile of it, undertaken within two years by the booksellers Payne and Foss, who acquired the volume and then on-sold it to the Duke of Devonshire, who possessed an immensely valuable library of early modern books. Payne and Foss seem to have taken for granted that the best way to present this newly unearthed quarto was through a type-facsimile, which they term 'an accurate reprint' (see Figures 23 and 24).

As Lesser explains, in a quite extraordinary twist (though one which seems appropriate for this most puzzling of all Shakespeare plays), where this copy of the quarto was missing its final page, a second copy was discovered in 1856 which lacked the title page but did have the final page. These remain the only two copies of the first quarto known to be in existence: the first is now in the Huntington Library and the second is at

---

[56] A. W. Pollard, '"Facsimile" Reprints of Old Books', *The Library* 6 (1926), 305–13, quotation at p. 311; see Smith, *Shakespeare's First Folio*, pp. 308–9.

[57] W. W. Greg, 'Type-Facsimiles and Others', *The Library* 6 (1926), 321–6, at p. 322.

[58] Zachary Lesser, *Hamlet after Q1: An Uncanny History of the Shakespearean Text* (Philadelphia: University of Pennsylvania Press, 2015).

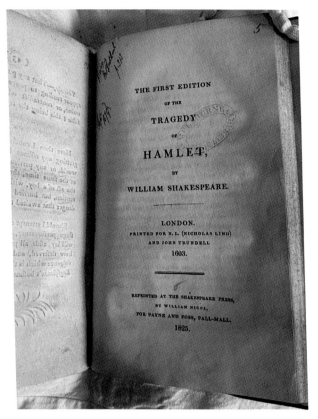

Figure 23 *First Edition of the Tragedy of Hamlet* (1825), State Library of
Victoria

the British Library. The excitement at the discovery of a new and substantially different text of *Hamlet* easily accounts for the rapidity with which the first discovered copy was made available as a facsimile, and this urgency was also evident when the second copy was also issued as a facsimile in 1858 – that is, just two years after it came to light.

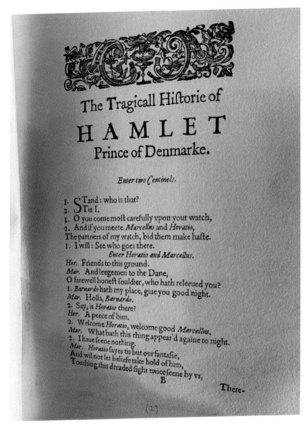

The Tragicall Historie of

H A M L E T

Prince of Denmarke.

Enter two Centinels.

1. STand: who is that?
2. STis I,
1. O you come most carefully vpon your watch,
2. And if you meete *Marcellus* and *Horatio*,
The partners of my watch, bid them make haste.
1. I will: See who goes there.
   Enter Horatio and Marcellus.
Hor. Friends to this ground.
Mar. And leegemen to the Dane,
O farewell honest souldier, who hath releeued you?
1. *Barnardo* hath my place, giue you good night.
Mar. Holla, *Barnardo*.
2. Say, is *Horatio* there?
Hor. A peece of him.
2. Welcome *Horatio*, welcome good *Marcellus*,
Mar. What hath this thing appear'd againe to night.
2. I haue seene nothing.
Mar. Horatio sayes tis but our fantasie,
And wil not let beliefe take hold of him,
Touching this dreaded sight twice seene by vs,

            B

                       There-

(1)

Figure 24 *First Edition of the Tragedy of Hamlet* (1825), State Library of Victoria

The first copy was acquired by the Duke of Devonshire, and a facsimile of it was overseen by J. P. Collier. It was printed using a process called photolithography, whereby a photograph was broken down into dots and transferred to a halftone screen, which could then be used as the base for multiple printings. (See Figure 25 for the State Library of Victoria's

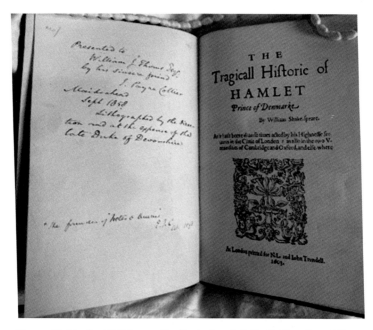

Figure 25 *Hamlet* Q1 lithographic facsimile ed. J. P. Collier, State Library of Victoria

presentation copy signed by Collier as a gift to William Thoms, a famous antiquarian and the founder of *Notes and Queries*.)

This volume is the first example of photolithography used to create a facsimile of an old book.[59] I discuss photographic facsimiles in detail in the next section, but it is important to recognize a kind of crossover moment as one process of textual reproduction (type-setting) gave way to another

---

[59] On this see Alan Galey, *The Shakespearean Archive: Experiments in New Media from the Renaissance to Postmodernity* (Cambridge: Cambridge University Press, 2014), pp. 135–42.

(photography). This transitional moment was a time when hand-traced facsimiles had their finest hour before giving way to less laborious processes. A type-facsimile required a certain amount of clever decision-making regarding typeface and layout – a kind of sleight of hand – by a printer to approximate to the extent possible the look of an original. On the other hand, traced facsimiles (whereby the text was reproduced by either tracing directly onto a lithographic stone, or transferred from tracing paper to a stone, or recreated individually for pages or sections of pages such as the work of John Harris, discussed in the Introduction) could, in theory, come even closer to the original, with the caveat that even traced facsimiles were, as with all printing of any kind, subject to human error.

This brings me to a particularly fascinating nineteenth-century editor and biographer of Shakespeare: James Orchard Halliwell Phillipps. Halliwell (who took his wife Henrietta's maiden name, Phillipps, later in life under the terms of her family will, despite having been disowned by Henrietta's father after James married her) came from a relatively modest background, and he carved out a career for himself which combined editorial work with book dealing.[60] Indeed, Halliwell was involved in a tangled financial transaction over the second copy of *Hamlet* Q1, first refusing to buy it from the Irish bookseller who had supposedly bought it from a student, then in the end paying even more to secure it from the London booksellers T. & W. Boone before on-selling it to the British Museum.[61] Halliwell was born in 1820, and by the time the second copy of *Hamlet* Q1 appeared, Halliwell, although still only thirty-six, had produced numerous editions of often obscure early modern works, as well as trading in originals. Always entrepreneurial, Halliwell carefully limited many of his editions to a small number of copies in order to increase the price through their scarcity.

---

[60] See the comprehensive biography by Marvin Spevack, *James Orchard Halliwell-Phillipps* (New Castle, DE: Oak Knoll Press, 2001). I also discuss Halliwell's editorial activities in *Editors Construct the Renaissance Canon, 1825–1915* (Cham: Palgrave Macmillan, 2018), chapter 3.

[61] See Lesser, *Hamlet after Q1*, pp. 23–4.

This is the case with a remarkable set of traced facsimiles of Shakespeare quartos, issued progressively during the 1860s. Halliwell organized this series of forty-eight facsimiles, but, as he admitted himself, the skill that brought them into being was embodied in the lithographer and engraver Edmund William Ashbee (not to be confused with the late nineteenth-century bibliographer and book collector Henry Spencer Ashbee). As Halliwell notes in the preface to the series: 'Every single letter has been traced from the originals by hand, and for all really practical uses, this series is as valuable as a collection of the early quartos themselves.'[62] Of course, this is in part a sales promotion, but there is no doubt that the traced facsimiles were extremely accurate, as well as being printed (single-sided) on high-quality paper (see Figure 26).

These quartos were produced at the very moment when the photographic facsimile was being pioneered, making them a key transitional medium for the reproduction of original copies of early modern books. Given that questions were raised from the start (and continue to be raised) about the reliability of photographic facsimiles, the Halliwell/Ashbee traced facsimile quartos assume in retrospect a kind of nostalgic aura: as epitomes of human craftsmanship, as opposed to technological advancement. Indeed, the craft element is also part of Halliwell's entrepreneurial approach to his publications, even if that went hand in hand with a genuine commitment to scholarship and utility. In the case of the quarto facsimiles series, this involved a carefully staged diminution of the number of copies as a strategy to increase their scarcity and accordingly their price. The quarto facsimiles were initially limited to a print run of fifty copies, with the lithograph plate then destroyed so that no further copies could be made. But the scarcity factor was dramatically increased by the decision to destroy nineteen copies so that only thirty-one would be available for sale (see Figure 27).

As an aside, it is worth remarking on the fact that the State Library of Victoria (SLV) in Melbourne, Australia, where I live, has a large proportion of the quarto facsimile set. The SLV has many quite rare volumes, but it is nevertheless unusual for this library to have one of only thirty-one copies of

---

[62] Quoted from Justin Winsor, *Halliwelliana* (Cambridge, MA: Harvard University Press, 1881), p. 20.

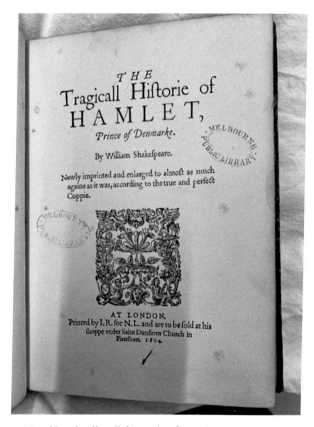

Figure 26 Ashbee/Halliwell facsimile of *Hamlet*, 1867, State Library of Victoria

a book, let alone the bulk of a set of such volumes. Even now, with access to many online facsimiles of Shakespeare quartos and other early modern texts, the experience of handling a high-end traced facsimile like the ones created by Ashbee and Halliwell remains valuable, a point I will return to in Section 10.

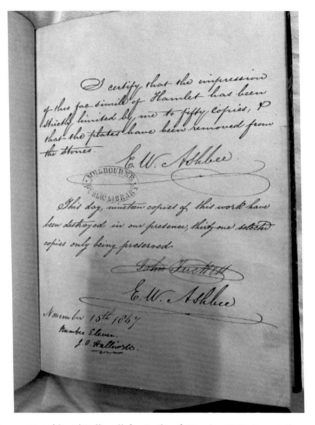

Figure 27 Ashbee/Halliwell facsimile of *Hamlet*, 1867, State Library of Victoria

3 The Photographic Era

Given how ubiquitous Halliwell was in every aspect of the trading and editing of early modern texts in the mid-nineteenth century, it is no surprise to find him at the very beginning of the photographic reproduction of books. In 1857, Halliwell experimented with the relatively new process of salted paper printing to produce a facsimile of the 1617 edition of *The Famous Victories of Henry the Fifth*. This technique involved placing a weak salt solution on paper, then coating it with one of a number of chemicals to allow it to take on an image, which was then stabilized by a second coating of salt solution. As discussed by Erin Blake on *The Collation*, the Folger Shakespeare Library's research blog, the resulting process was not very successful because the images began to fade almost immediately. As Blake notes, the copy in the Boston Public Library was already registered as faded in 1878.[63] (As is so often the case with Halliwell, the production run of this facsimile was limited to ten copies to increase its value.)

More successful experiments with a photographic process for facsimiles were carried out at the Ordnance Survey as an offshoot of the Survey's interest in the relationship between photography and cartography. The process was instituted by Howard Staunton, who was until then more prominent as a chess player and commentator than as an editor, though he produced a complete edition of Shakespeare between 1858 and 1860.[64] In 1861, Staunton had the Survey reproduce the first 162 pages of the first folio as an experiment using photographic zincography. (Put simply, zincography is a printing process that uses zinc plates instead of the limestone used in lithography.) The Ordnance Survey specialized in the use of zincography, but Staunton, in the end, had a complete folio facsimile produced by the printers Day and Son using photographic lithography. The facsimile was published in 1866. The title page underlines the technical process and also the sources, which were evidently both the British Museum copy and the Bridgewater copy of the first folio (see Figure 28).

While the Ashbee/Halliwell traced facsimiles of the quartos were a considerable achievement and endure as a legacy of that methodology, the photographic facsimile of the first folio pointed to a long but controversial history of attempts to get as close as possible to an original text. In

---

[63] Erin Blake, 'A Photographic Facsimile from 1857', *The Collation* (https://collation.folger.edu/2017/07/photographic-facsimile-from-1857, accessed 12 April 2022).

[64] For a brief account, see Franklin B. Williams Jr, 'Photo-Facsimiles of "STC" Books: A Cautionary Check List', *Studies in Bibliography* 21 (1968): 109–30.

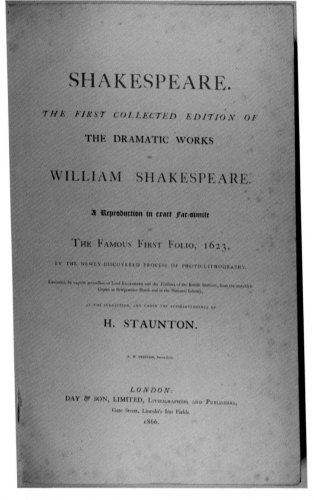

Figure 28 Staunton photolithographic facsimile of first folio, 1866, Harry Ransom Center, PR 2751 A15 1866

his groundbreaking book on the relationship between Shakespeare and technological change through time, Alan Galey notes, 'The nineteenth century was the first great age of facsimiles and other forms of documentary reproduction, and the rise of the photographic facsimile in the mid-to-late nineteenth century parallels the more recent rise of digitization projects such as *Early English Books Online* (*EEBO*).'[65] I take up the relationship between photographic and online facsimiles in Section 8, but for now I want to concentrate on Galey's argument that already with nineteenth-century photographic facsimiles we can see an oscillation between the elation at purportedly flawless replication, and an anxiety over that idea being a misrepresentation. The accuracy of this mode of textual reproduction even generated anxiety over what it might mean to achieve perfect replication. Galey argues that, if the advent of photography produced something like a seismic shift in the way knowledge was organized, then the photographic facsimile encouraged a new way of understanding the role of textual history in Shakespeare studies.

Galey emphasizes that the Collier photographic facsimile of *Hamlet* Q1 (discussed in Section 2) included the last page from the British Museum copy, missing in the Devonshire copy from which the rest of the facsimile was photographed.[66] The result, however 'accurate' a reproduction, is not a replica of a single original object, but rather a new creation based on two originals. The final result is, one can speculate, prompted by a desire to have a more complete text than the two which survived, because the British Museum copy, while having the last page that is missing in the Devonshire copy, lacks the title page, which is present in the Devonshire copy. This is therefore not an act of historical preservation, but rather an act of recreation. This act is thus not unlike the habit of 'perfecting' early modern books, especially Shakespeare volumes, that might have a missing, or torn, or stained page, through a process that usually, in the nineteenth century, involved the insertion of a hand-drawn or -traced work.[67] Collier also, as

---

[65] Galey, *Shakespearean Archive*, p. 119. [66] Ibid., p. 141.

[67] On perfecting in relation to the first folio, see Smith, *Shakespeare's First Folio*, chapter 5, and on Halliwell's approach to perfecting, see Salzman, *Editors Construct the Renaissance Canon*, pp. 71–2.

part of the proofing of the photographed pages, cleaned up the copy, including, for example, removing the apparent inking out of 'Oxford' on the title page so that the entire title is pristine.[68]

Perfecting is indeed significant for the evolution of facsimiles, although it was confined to small parts of a book rather than the replication of an entire text. As the nineteenth-century evaluation of a few medieval and early modern texts as iconic grew, so too did the yearning among some collectors for copies that had no missing pages, no signs of the wear and tear that inevitably occurred through the passage of time. This is where those who sold rare books, like Halliwell, resorted to a series of measures to 'perfect' a copy in a way that would make it worth more. For Halliwell, this often meant cannibalizing his 'excess' copies of volumes (including Shakespeare folios!) by cutting out the required pages and using them to replace damaged pages, or to make up missing ones, in a copy he was selling.[69] An alternative was either to touch up or create whole facsimile pages for this kind of perfecting, often using the hand-drawn or -traced method exemplified by the Harris example mentioned in the Introduction. Furthermore, with the advent of photography, it was possible to use the kind of sorting process of picking out 'best' pages that would continue through to a twentieth-century example like the Hinman folio facsimile, discussed in Section 4.

The idea that a book could be perfected using a possibly undetectable (to all but the most trained eyes) facsimile illustrates perfectly some of the anxiety, as well as accomplishment, that Galey discusses in his analysis of the impact of photographic facsimiles. Galey notes with characteristic acuity: 'As the Victorians were learning how to read photographs, one of the possible responses was faith in the photograph's indexical relation to the real, though Collier's facsimile could more accurately be described as

---

[68] I owe this observation to a suggestion by Zachary Lesser.

[69] Again on this topic see Smith, Chapter 5, and Salzman, *Editors Construct the Renaissance Canon*, pp. 71–2, but see also the detailed description of examples in individual first folios in Eris Rasmussen and Anthony James West, *The Shakespeare First Folios: A Descriptive Catalogue* (Cham: Palgrave Macmillan, 2011).

having an indexical relation to the virtual.'[70] Galey points out how one significant effect of the trust placed in photographic facsimiles was the consolidation of the idea that a reader who owned a facsimile could look past the thick accumulation of editorial commentary and emendations, and instead access the original and undiluted Shakespeare text.[71] However, as Galey goes on to explain, both the photographic facsimile and the heavily annotated edition illustrate what he calls 'late Victorian archival fantasies' – that is, an imagined world of complete and ordered knowledge.[72] The facsimile feeds into this fantasy by allowing possession of apparent replicas of otherwise unobtainable originals, so completeness (that ever receding goal of all collectors) can be reached.

The Ordnance Survey approach to photographic facsimiles began with a variety of examples, including historical texts such as the Domesday Book and Magna Carta, so the field stretched much wider than just Shakespeare. As David McKitterick explains in reference to the rise of photographic facsimiles, the Ordnance Office set the precedent for producing facsimiles of manuscripts, but '[p]hotolithography was a process better suited to the sharp contrasts of black and white in printed texts than to the reproduction of different densities of ink in manuscripts'.[73] Nevertheless, photographic facsimiles did not become widely available until later in the century, when they, once again, concentrated on Shakespeare. This coincided with ever cheaper editions of Shakespeare. At the same time, as McKitterick notes, the advent of photographic facsimiles did not drive out type-facsimiles entirely, with a number of early modern books receiving notable facsimile treatment from the publisher Elliot Stock.[74] Stock produced high-quality type-facsimiles of *Paradise Lost*, Herbert's *The Temple*, Walton's *Compleat Angler*, and Defoe's *Robinson Crusoe*, though McKitterick notes that later editions of *Pilgrim's*

---

[70] Galey, *Shakespearean Archive*, p. 142. [71] Ibid., p. 153. [72] Ibid.

[73] McKitterick, *Old Books, New Technologies*, p. 126. For a detailed and comprehensive account of the development of lithography, with a concentration on art, see Michael Twyman, *Early Lithographed Books* (London: Farrand Press and Private Libraries, 1990), and *Breaking the Mould: The First Hundred Years of Lithography* (London: British Library, 2001).

[74] McKitterick, *Old Books, New Technologies*, pp. 131–2.

Progress and *Religio Medici* were more like faux early modern volumes than facsimiles.[75] The involvement of Alexander Grosart in this process is especially interesting because Grosart is responsible for a veritable avalanche of editions of early modern literature late in the nineteenth century. I will return to this aspect of his career later, but for now it is worth noting Grosart's introduction to the type-facsimile of Herbert's *The Temple* (see Figure 29).

In the course of his discussion, which offers detailed information about the bibliographical background to Herbert's posthumous collection, Grosart boasts about the quality of the facsimile while calling this volume a vital tool in establishing Herbert's true place in the literary canon: 'The little volume now reproduced in absolute fac-simile in every way – viz., in type, paper, binding – apart from its own preciousness, in its own humble but most genuine kind, holds a memorable place in our literary biography.'[76] It is worth noting that even in the introduction, the type, while modern, uses the long S and ligatures (joining the long S to the next letter) as a kind of signal of either quaint antiquarianism or fidelity to the original, depending upon your level of sympathy with this kind of project. The quality of the type-facsimile is indeed high, although, at least in the copies I have examined, paper and binding are nothing like their early modern counterparts, and certainly nothing like as wedded to replication as, say, the Smeeton *Solimon and Perseda* (see Figures 30A and 30B).

Despite this ongoing production of type-facsimiles, photographic facsimiles reached a much wider market later in the century with a series initiated by F. J. Furnivall. Furnivall founded a whole series of literary societies, including the Early English Text Society, a highly influential organization dedicated to publishing editions of early literature which is, remarkably, still in existence and still publishing valuable editions.[77] (Unfortunately, Furnivall was an exceptionally irascible society member and became involved in many feuds.) Furnivall was part of the Victorian movement to bring education to the working class, an idea that underlay a number of his publishing ventures, but he also had the ability to experiment with editorial techniques, so that, for

---

[75] Ibid., pp. 136–7.

[76] George Herbert, *The Temple*, ed Alexander B. Grosart (1876), long S changed to normal S.

[77] See the Society's webpage: https://users.ox.ac.uk/~eets/index.html.

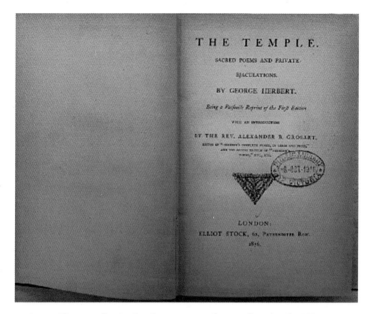

Figure 29 Type-facsimile of George Herbert, *The Temple*, 1876, State
Library of Victoria.

example, his multiple-source, six-text edition of Chaucer remains influential
to this day.[78] Furnivall was instrumental in organizing an ambitious series of
photographic facsimiles of Shakespeare's quartos, a series that could be seen
as the photographic equivalent of the Halliwell/Ashbee traced facsimiles, but
produced with an aim to be more affordable and, in theory at least, more
accurate. The series took more than a decade to complete (1880–91) and ran
to forty-three volumes. Just as Ashbee was acknowledged by Halliwell to be

[78] See William S. Peterson, 'Furnivall, Frederick James (1825–1910), Textual
Scholar and Editor', *Oxford Dictionary of National Biography*. 23 Sep. 2004
(accessed 5 November 2022). For more on Furnivall as editor, see Salzman,
Editors Construct the Renaissance Canon, pp. 94–9.

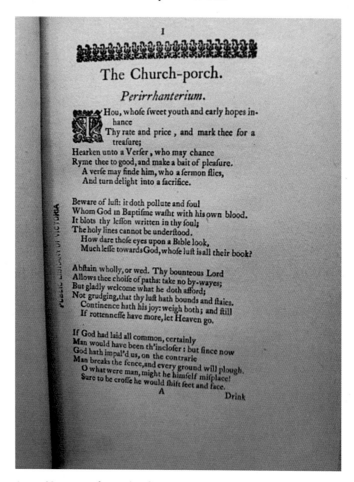

I

The Church-porch.

Perirrhanterium.

Hou, whofe fweet youth and early hopes in-
hance
Thy rate and price , and mark thee for a
treafure;
Hearken unto a Verfer , who may chance
Ryme thee to good, and make a bait of pleafure.
   A verfe may finde him, who a fermon flies,
   And turn delight into a facrifice.

Beware of luft: it doth pollute and foul
Whom God in Baptifme wafht with his own blood.
It blots thy leffon written in thy foul;
The holy lines cannot be underftood.
   How dare thofe eyes upon a Bible look,
   Much leffe towards God, whofe luft is all their book?

Abftain wholly, or wed. Thy bounteous Lord
Allows thee choife of paths: take no by-wayes;
But gladly welcome what he doth afford;
Not grudging, that thy luft hath bounds and ftaies.
   Continence hath his joy: weigh both; and ftill
   If rottenneffe have more, let Heaven go.

If God had laid all common, certainly
Man would have been th'inclofer : but fince now
God hath impal'd us, on the contrarie
Man breaks the fence, and every ground will plough.
   O what were man, might he himfelf mifplace!
   Sure to be croffe he would fhift feet and face.

A

Drink

Figure 30A Type-facsimile of George Herbert, *The Temple*, 1876, State
Library of Victoria, p. 1

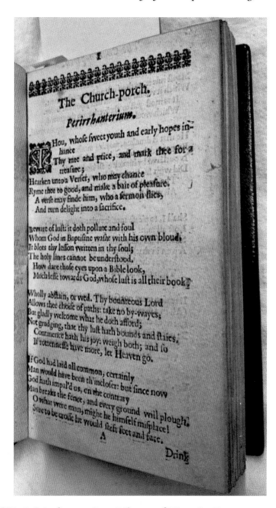

Figure 30B Original page, State Library of Victoria, Emmerson Collection

the true hero of the traced facsimile series, so William Griggs and then, after 1886, Charles Praetorius, the photo-lithographers, were the true heroes of this later series.[79] Starting out at six shillings, each volume was a bargain in comparison with the expensive and extremely limited Ashbee/Halliwell series. While the photographic reproduction is generally of a high quality (volumes 150 odd years on retain excellent clarity), there were innovative additions to the text to help navigation, notably the marginal insertion of act and scene number and of line numbers, as can be seen, for example, in the Q2 *Hamlet* volume (see Figures 31 and 32).

Here we can see the marginal act and scene numbers and line numbers which, taken together with Furnivall's introduction, allow for a scholarly engagement with the text, as well as assisting general readers in navigating the play. This series takes us to the end of the nineteenth century and towards a significant moment for facsimiles with the emergence of what has been called the New Bibliography, and the interactions between bibliography, textual scholarship, editing, and the technological capacity for facsimile production.

4 New Bibliography, New Facsimiles

A revolution in bibliographical knowledge occurred at the beginning of the twentieth century. I do not want to spend too much time going into the complex and often opaque specialist discussions about bibliography and textual editing, but some knowledge of them is required because these discussions both centred on Shakespeare and involved, if at times peripherally, ideas about the requirements for facsimiles.[80] Given the history I have been outlining here, it is important to stress that, while early twentieth-century editors tended to claim that they represented an almost scientific advance on the editorial practices of the nineteenth century, this

---

[79] See Franklin B. Williams Jr, 'Photo-Facsimiles of "STC" Books: A Cautionary Check List', *Studies in Bibliography* 21 (1968): 112–13.

[80] For an excellent (if at times controversial) summary of these issues, see Gabriel Egan, *The Struggle for Shakespeare's Text: Twentieth-Century Editorial Theory and Practice* (Cambridge: Cambridge University Press, 2010).

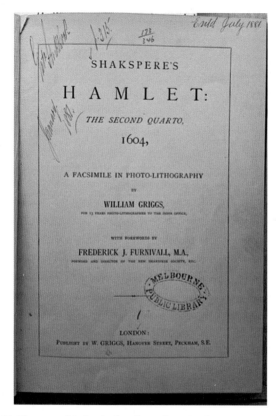

Figure 31 Photographic facsimile of *Hamlet* Q2, ed. F. J. Furnivall, 1881,
State Library of Victoria

was rather exaggerated, and there have been more measured assessments of
late that give the eighteenth- and nineteenth-century editors their due.[81]

---

[81] See, for example, Jeremy Lopez, *Constructing the Canon of Early Modern Drama*
(Cambridge: Cambridge University Press, 2014); Salzman, *Editors Construct the
Renaissance Canon*, and Galey, *Shakespearean Archive*.

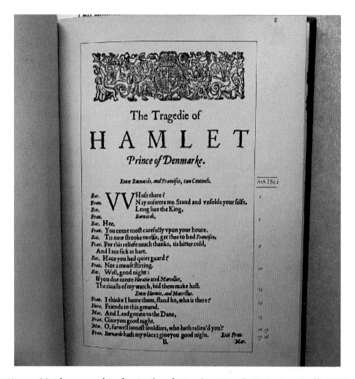

Figure 32 Photographic facsimile of *Hamlet* Q2, ed. F. J. Furnivall, 1881, State Library of Victoria

The New Bibliography created a much greater knowledge of early modern printing and transmission processes, but it can also be seen as the logical late stage of the approach to establishing a reliable author figure, and an increased attention to the earliest surviving texts, that Margreta de Grazia outlines in her argument about the establishment of those critical factors at the end of the eighteenth century (and that I discussed in Section 1).[82] It is

[82] See de Grazia, *Shakespeare Verbatim.*

also worth noting that one of the key early examples of new ideas behind New Bibliography was an edition, not of Shakespeare, but of the Elizabethan writer of many genres, but only one play, Thomas Nashe. The editor in question was R. B. McKerrow. McKerrow, along with A. W. Pollard, was a foundational member of the Bibliographical Society. He initially worked in publishing but then became an academic, writing the extremely influential *An Introduction to Bibliography for Literary Students* in 1927.

McKerrow's edition of Nashe allowed him scope to begin to set out theories of editing that included the influential idea of choosing a 'copy text' as the foundation of an edition, and then mapping the deviations from it in later versions of the same work. McKerrow explains this in the textual introduction to Volume One of the Nashe edition: 'The spelling of the copy-text, by which, here and throughout the book, I mean the text used in each particular case as the basis of mine, has been followed exactly except as regards evident misprints.'[83] While much of what followed on from McKerrow's insights was directed at a greater understanding of the publication of Shakespeare, the New Bibliographers were, like some of the nineteenth-century editors before them, careful to analyse and edit an enormous range of early modern printed works. This is especially the case with the third and perhaps most esteemed figure from this period, W. W. Greg. Greg made extensive use of facsimiles in his influential 1931 study, *Dramatic Documents from the Elizabethan Playhouses*.[84] In this, Greg followed in the footsteps of James Orchard Halliwell Phillipps, who, as I have discussed previously, also used facsimiles in a variety of imaginative ways, not just in his series of play editions, but also in his assemblages of documents and material especially relating to Shakespeare's biography.

For the purposes of my study, however, the triumvirate of McKerrow, Pollard, and Greg was instrumental not just in theorizing bibliography and

---

[83] R. B. McKerrow, ed., *The Works of Thomas Nashe* (1904, rpt London: Sidgwick and Jackson, 1910), vol 1, p. xi.

[84] W. W. Greg, *Dramatic Documents from the Elizabethan Playhouses*, 2 vols. (Oxford: Oxford University Press, 1931).

textual editing, but, through the Malone Society, in producing facsimiles of a large range of early modern and medieval texts, as well as influencing ideas for a new Shakespeare edition. Facsimiles took on a new importance for the New Bibliographers because such documents allowed (with care) for the more extensive analysis of the individual plays, and individual copies of those plays, that was essential for an approach to editing which stressed close attention to primary sources and to extensive collation.[85] Greg gradually formulated a role for the editor which allowed for considerable, albeit informed, decision-making, in an attempt to produce a text that might be closer to the author's intentions than what is evident in any single source. Following on from Greg, the American bibliographer Fredson Bowers, founder of the journal *Studies in Bibliography*, emphasized even further the idea that the editor might be able to see through the extant textual material to the manuscript 'original' – an idea much disputed, as will be discussed in Section 9.[86] But even at an earlier stage of the ideas being formulated by New Bibliography, the stress on informed editorial intervention meant that the facsimile could be a source of information in the absence of the original, rather than a viable reading or performing text – something that was to be challenged later in the century.

This is a moment at the beginning of the twentieth century when the Malone Society offered a carefully considered programme of facsimiles aimed at the scholarly market, while at the same time a continuation of the nineteenth-century connoisseurs/collectors market was still being cultivated. The Malone Society was Pollard's initiative, and the purpose of its facsimiles, as Greg explained retrospectively, was 'that work of permanent utility can be done by placing in the hand of students at large such reproductions of the original textual authorities as may make constant and

---

[85] For a particularly ingenious account of how New Bibliography's textual theories had to be adapted to a period when travel was restricted, as opposed to the FIFO (Fly In Fly Out) style of academic existence in the 1970s and 1980s, see Sarah Neville, 'The Accidentals Tourist: Greg's "Rationale of Copy-Text" and the Dawn of Transatlantic Air Travel', *Textual Cultures* 14 (2021): 18–29.

[86] Fredson Bowers, *On Editing Shakespeare and the Elizabethan Dramatists* (Philadelphia: University of Pennsylvania Library, 1955).

continuous reference to the originals unnecessary'.[87] As discussed earlier in my account of *Solimon and Perseda*, the Malone Society motto ('the permanent utility of original texts') assumed that the most useful facsimile was closer to an edition than to a reproduction, hence the paradox inherent in 'original'. In order to unpack this, I need to return to Greg's formulation that 'photographic reproductions are reliable but illegible, reprints are legible but unreliable'.[88] Greg goes on to explain how a type-facsimile, at least those carefully prepared for the Malone Society publications, can be based on a partial collation:

> '[B]y comparing several copies of the original, it is often possible to determine a reading which in one particular copy, or indeed in each several copy, may be open to doubt. Here again the reprint, which is able to collate evidence, has the pull over the reproduction that can reproduce only the data of a single copy.'[89]

This idea would be challenged by the Hinman first folio facsimile, which did not reproduce a single original, but rather pages from numbers of originals. I will return to this point. However, Greg here offers a carefully thought-out rationale for the type-facsimile which will be something more like an edition, even if it is intended to adhere closely to the original. Greg notes that the Malone Society facsimiles 'do not profess to be . . . absolutely rigorous facsimiles'.[90] So, unlike some of the nineteenth-century type-facsimiles discussed earlier, which strove for absolute aesthetic accuracy, the Malone Society was not trying to replicate type, spacing, or page size, let alone paper, but rather it offered a facsimile that might be described as truer to content than to form. This shift reflects the divided market for editions in the early twentieth century: the Malone Society's publications are directed at students and scholars, rather than at collectors or connoisseurs.

The first set of Malone Society facsimiles was published in 1907, with Greg solely responsible for five of the six volumes. The volumes varied

---

[87] W. W. Greg, 'Type-Facsimiles and Others', *The Library* 6 (1926): 321.
[88] Ibid., p. 322. [89] Ibid. [90] Ibid., p. 325.

from non-canonical but not wholly obscure Elizabethan plays like Peele's *The Battle of Alcaʒar* (1594) and Greene's *Orlando Furioso* (also 1594), to two mid-sixteenth-century interludes.[91] *The Battle of Alcaʒar* is a good example of the care Greg devoted to the enterprise. It has a photographic reproduction of the original title page and a detailed textual introduction, where Greg explains that he has collated two copies and consulted two others in dealing with a carelessly printed text. A sample page shows the advantages of the Malone Society type-facsimile methodology for a text like this one: it is not a reproduction of the original, as I have been noting, but a kind of faithful transcript, with added line numbers, but with all the original spelling, punctuation, stage directions, and so on, usually described as a 'diplomatic transcription' (see Figure 33).

As well as printed plays, the Malone Society facsimiles included manuscripts, perhaps the most interesting early example being Jane Lumley's translation of Euripides' *Iphegenia*, which Greg edited in 1909. In the nineteenth century, traced facsimiles of manuscripts would have been difficult to produce, and the comparative scarcity of type-facsimiles can be accounted for by the focus on Shakespeare and associated drama. The more even balance between manuscript and print witnesses with the Malone type-facsimile series is notable. For example, the fascinating manuscript of *The Second Maiden's Tragedy* was again edited by Greg in 1910. As I noted in my discussion of *Solimon and Perseda*, the Malone Society facsimile series has the honour of being the longest-running facsimile series, with a number of titles still being published every year.

At almost the same time as the Malone Society facsimile series, John Stephen Farmer was publishing a series of collotype facsimiles of early modern texts in a manner more reminiscent of the nineteenth-century series by someone like Halliwell Phillipps. (As explained earlier, the collotype method avoids half tone screens, and is a much clearer, albeit more time-consuming and expensive, photographic reproductive process.) Farmer was a fascinating figure who, in the 1880s and 1890s, published a series of works

---

[91] The Society has a helpful, downloadable complete list of its editions on its website: https://malonesociety.com/wp-content/uploads/2019/06/Malone-Publications-List-2019.pdf.

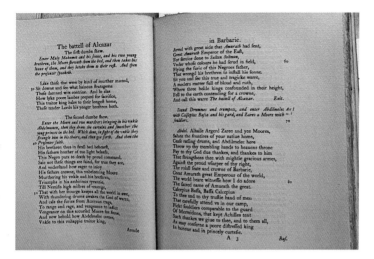

Figure 33 George Peele, *The Battle of Alcaʒar*, ed. W. W. Greg, Malone Society, 1907, State Library of Victoria

on spiritualism and on slang.[92] Farmer moved on to editions of early plays in 1905 and then in 1907 began the Tudor Facsimile Texts series. Over the next seven years, Farmer published 184 facsimile volumes, many of them containing plays that were obscure and only extant in a few copies. As noted early in this Element in relation to the *Solimon and Perseda* facsimile, in choosing collotype photographic reproduction, Farmer was opting for the clearest and most accurate photographic facsimile method available. In an advertisement designed to allure buyers, which doubles as an important account of how the series was produced, Farmer stated that his facsimiles would show 'the original as it actually exists today; in which is preserved all

---

[92] Farmer has no ODNB entry, though he certainly deserves one. Biographical information is contained in Patrick J. Kearney's online bibliography: http://scissors-and-paste.net/pdf/Farmer.pdf.

the detail of size, imperfect type, and the imperfections in the paper, even to stains and "mendings", and, when possible, the natural discoloration due to age'.[93] Farmer goes on to note the high reputation of 'Mr. R. Fleming, a technical photographer of many years' experience', as well as stating that the facsimiles have been compared with the originals by 'Mr. J. A. Herbert, of the Manuscript department of the British Museum'.[94] It is especially worth noting that, unlike the standard size format of the Malone Society facsimiles, Farmer adjusts the volume size of his facsimiles to match the originals, so while the published plays are generally quarto, some, like the especially useful facsimile of Massinger's autograph manuscript of *Believe As You List*, are much larger. While Farmer's series is less accessible than the Malone series, it remains a valuable resource for those either without access to *Early English Books Online* (*EEBO*) or who want to consult a book rather than an online facsimile – always bearing in mind the cautionary tale of the *Solimon and Perseda* facsimile.

These two facsimile series exemplify the state of play at the beginning of the twentieth century, with the Malone type-facsimiles epitomizing the careful approach to editing being put into place by New Bibliographers like Greg, and the continued courting of the antiquarian market illustrated by Farmer's collotype series. The next stage of development saw the incorporation of New Bibliographic principles into the photographic facsimile, while the twentieth century was gradually approaching the developments that ultimately led to online facsimiles.

5 The Hinman Folio Facsimile and Reproduction As a Manipulated Ideal Text

Gabriel Egan has outlined in painstaking detail how New Bibliography began to focus on the minute particulars of printing practices in order to understand how Shakespeare's works were constructed.[95] The figure who

---

[93] John S. Farmer, *A Handlist to the Tudor Facsimile Texts* (1914), preface.
[94] Ibid.
[95] Egan, *Struggle for Shakespeare's Text*, pp. 72–9. For an expansive account of Hinman and his collator, see Steven Escar Smith, "'The Eternal Verities

most influenced this trend was Charlton Hinman, who devoted himself to collating and then analysing the seventy-nine copies of the first folio available at the time that formed part of the Folger Shakespeare Library's expansive collection. Hinman undertook this task for two main reasons: (1) to locate the work of various compositors (the workers who set type by hand, starting by fitting the individual pieces of type into a composing stick, hence the name compositor) as they set type for the folio; and (2) as a way of tracing the corrections that for early modern books were made during the process of printing, so that formes (groups of typeset pages printed on individual sheets of paper) or pages, would vary according to whether they were corrected or uncorrected. Hinman published an extremely detailed study of this process.[96] However, Hinman also used some of this information to inform the massive photographic facsimile of the first folio which he had undertaken to publish. As Egan and other scholars have noted, the Hinman first folio facsimile was unusual in so far as it was based, not on reproduction of a single copy of the folio; nor, as was the case with some nineteenth-century examples, was it based on two. Rather, Hinman chose what he considered to be the best pages from a large number of first folios in the Folger's collection. He was thus involved in a version of the perfecting process that I discussed earlier in this Element – that is, he was assembling a single facsimile that 'fixed up' the errors, blurred type, stains, and other 'imperfect' aspects of individual pages that any single source copy would contain. The result was a facsimile that represented as close to an 'ideal'

Verified": Charlton Hinman and the Roots of Mechanical Collation', *Studies in Bibliography* 53 (2000): 129–61.

[96] Charlton Hinman, *The Printing and Proof-Reading of the First Folio of Shakespeare*, 2 vols. (Oxford: Clarendon, 1963); for a remarkable account linking the American New Bibliographers' rhetoric about the identities of compositors and the contemporaneous American obsession with searching out and type-casting (pun intended) homosexuality, see Jeffrey Masten, 'Pressing Subjects or, The Secret Lives of Shakespeare's Compositors', in Jeffrey Masten, Peter Stallybrass, and Nancy J. Vickers, eds., *Language Machines: Technologies of Literary and Cultural Production* (New York: Routledge, 1997), pp. 75–107; and *Queer Philologies: Sex, Language, and Affect in Shakespeare's Time* (Philadelphia: University of Pennsylvania Press, 2016), chapter 1.

copy of the first folio as possible – a book that did not actually exist in real life.

Hinman established his ideas about the kind of facsimile he wanted to create in an essay on the Halliwell Phillipps facsimile, which he published in *Shakespeare Quarterly* in 1954.[97] Halliwell had written an introduction to the 1876 first folio facsimile, which was published by Chatto and Windus in a reduced-size format (see Figure 34).

As Hinman notes, Halliwell's facsimile was popular through to the twentieth century because of its convenient size and perceived reliability. However, Hinman points out that approximately the first half of the Halliwell facsimile reproduces an original folio that was purchased by the publishers, but the rest is in fact a reproduction of the Staunton facsimile, which itself is based on two separate copies. Hinman is able to trace this process because of his efforts to collate the Folger's copies, and doing so enabled him to identify individual pages (at various stages of stop-press correction) from individual copies of the folio. More seriously, Hinman notes that the photographic process involved many examples of cleaning up and intended correction, a process which, as Hinman details, actually introduced errors. (This process was achieved, as I have discussed earlier, through 'corrections' made to the lithograph before it was printed.) Hinman has many examples of this process, some minor, some radical, such as changing 'Tunne-dish' to 'Tunnerdish', or 'want' to 'went'.[98] This is, as I have already noted, following Alan Galey, a key aspect of the ambiguity surrounding photographic facsimiles: we read the photographic facsimile as an exact reproduction because it hides its origins, and in the case of a large and complex book like the folio, only a collation like Hinman's picks up those origins.

Hinman's own facsimile project carried some of the same ambiguities, but, in Hinman's case, he made them explicit. Hinman used his collation of all the Folger first folios to choose what he thought to be the best individual pages to photograph. For Hinman, this meant that his facsimile would be

---

[97] Charlton Hinman, 'The "Halliwell-Phillipps Facsimile" of the First Folio of Shakespeare', *Shakespeare Quarterly* 5 (1954): 395–401.

[98] Ibid., p. 399.

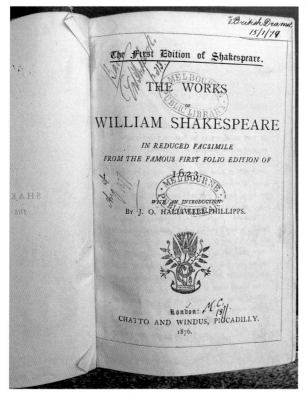

Figure 34 'Halliwell-Phillipps' reduced-size folio facsimile, 1876, State Library of Victoria

a kind of historical reconstruction, not of any folio that actually existed, but rather of a perfect or ideal folio. Hinman explains this idea in his preface:

> The primary aim of the present facsimile is to furnish a reliable photographic reproduction of what the printers of the original edition would themselves have considered an

ideal copy of the First Folio of Shakespeare: one in which
every page is not only clear and readable throughout but
represents the latest or most fully corrected state of the
text.[99]

As Egan explains, this could be seen as the culmination of a New
Bibliography dream of recreating the author's (or in this case the printer's)
ideal, intended text; as Egan puts it, 'Hinman's folio facsimile of 1968
represents the high water mark of a certain kind of idealization about
early modern printing.'[100] Hinman's process also recalls the techniques of
perfecting early modern books in the nineteenth century, especially valuable ones like the first folio, by supplying missing pages or replacing
damaged ones with pages from another copy or with a facsimile page.
Hinman perfected his folio facsimile by leveraging his ability to choose
which pages got photographed from which copies, in the same way that
Halliwell Phillipps perfected a folio by removing damaged pages and
tipping in 'better' ones. The Hinman facsimile is thus a kind of monument
to Hinman's process of reconstructing how the first folio came into being;
even if the reconstruction has been challenged as time went on for obscuring
the realities of early modern printing, it remains a remarkable piece of
painstaking scholarship and editing.

Hinman's facsimile has a scholarly scaffolding because he explains
exactly what choices he has made and how he has made them. As with
all facsimiles, it is possible to see the compromises and limitations of this
particular example, especially in retrospect. Hinman in his preface
explains that, although he consulted seventy-nine copies from the
Folger's collection, he ended up using thirty of those copies to make the
facsimile, with just two copies accounting for nearly a third of all the pages

---

[99] *The Norton Facsimile: The First Folio of Shakespeare*, prepared by Charlton
Hinman (London: Paul Hamlyn, 1968), p. xxii.

[100] Egan, *Struggle for Shakespeare's Text*, p. 79; and see the excellent article by
Joseph A. Dane, '"Ideal Copy" versus "Ideal Texts": The Application of
Bibliographical Description to Facsimiles', *Papers of the Bibliographical Society
of Canada* 33 (1995): 31–50.

reproduced. Hinman provides an appendix listing which copy was photographed for each page. More importantly, in contrast with some predecessors, Hinman assures us that no touching-up or correction process was used for the photography. One obvious way in which the page of the facsimile is not identical to the same page in the original is that Hinman supplies marginal line numbers, which are numbered consecutively, but begin afresh for each play (see Figure 35).

Hinman points out that at the time he published the facsimile there was no standard reference system for Shakespeare's plays other than act and scene references often linked back to the nineteenth-century Globe edition. Such references could not be standardized because act and scene divisions varied from edition to edition. So Hinman's through-line numbering system for each play was extremely practical and is still commonly used by scholars when citing the first folio. At the foot of the page Hinman prints act and scene numbers for the play, but also the page number of the facsimile. Such a system does change the appearance and also, we could say, the affect of the facsimile page, affording a greater sense of where one is in the play, compared to a more freely shifting sense if one reads an actual copy of the folio. The photographed pages are also inset into the pages of the facsimile, which has the advantage of allowing the reader to 'see' the entire original page, but the page of the facsimile has a different dimension to the page of the original. Because of this, the facsimile is even larger than the already very substantial folio. (While the sizes of individual folio copies vary, they are generally 12 to 13 inches high and 8 inches wide, compared to the Hinman facsimile, which is 14 inches high and 9 inches wide.) Hinman explains that the pages were reproduced by 'fine-screen (133-line) offset plates made from glossy photographs'.[101] (One hundred and thirty-three lines per inch is a sharper process than the more standard 100 lines per inch.)

The standard of reproduction for the Hinman facsimile may be very high, but it is worth noting that the folio was photographed in black and white, not in colour. This is significant and, of course, was also the case with all the preceding photographic facsimiles. The fact that these facsimiles are not in

---

[101] *Norton Facsimile*, p. xxiii.

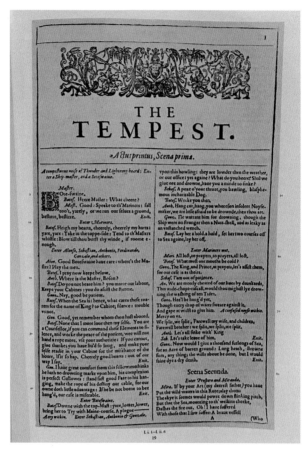

Figure 35 Charlton Hinman, Norton facsimile

colour is easily overlooked, as it is usual to think of books as generally being printed in black ink on white paper. However, early modern books were at the start printed on paper that varied greatly in shade, with ink that was also variable even within the same book object.[102] The paper that most of these books were printed on was made from rags, pulped, and then pressed through a wire mould, a process that nearly always produced watermarks: symbols that formed part of the mould to identify the papermaker or source of the paper. Watermarks are generally only visible when held up to the light – this means photographs nearly always fail to show them.[103] Similarly, ink was made from linseed oil and lampblack, and varied considerably from batch to batch. Over time, the colour of both pages and ink changed, often quite dramatically, in a way that black-and-white photography could not capture, just as much as that photography tended not to have contrast sharp enough to pick up small things like the difference between a punctuation mark and a stain, or even the clarity to detect the exact contours of an individual letter of type that was worn or damaged. The end result is that a black-and-white photographic facsimile stands at a considerable distance from the original. Still, though, these facsimiles were produced, like the originals they claimed to reproduce, as books. The next revolution in reproduction, while continuing to strive for a certain accuracy, however tempered by some of the issues outlined here, moved from the three dimensions of a codex, to the two-dimensionality of a microfilm image.

6 The Microfilm Revolution

Microfilm's history in some ways runs parallel to the history of photography. Microfilm was developed from the miniature photograph, invented by John Dancer in 1839, and then turned into film by the French optician René Dagron. The use of microfilm as an extremely effective way to store data, such as bank records and subsequently newspapers, was established in the

---

[102] For an excellent brief account, which is an invaluable summary of the whole process of producing and analysing early modern printed books, see Sarah Werner, *Studying Early Printed Books: 1450–1800* (Chichester: Wiley Blackwell, 2019). See also Philip Gaskell, *A New Introduction to Bibliography* (New Castle, DE: Oak Knoll Press, 2015), p. 57.

[103] For a detailed example of the use of watermarks in Shakespeare studies and bibliography, see Emma Depledge, 'False Dating: The Case of the "1676" *Hamlet* Quartos', *Papers of the Bibliographical Society of America* 112 (2018): 183–99.

1920s, and further developed with improvements in cameras in the 1930s. As far as facsimiles are concerned, however, the key moment is in 1938 when Eugene Power founded University Microfilms and set about photographing all the items in the Pollard and Redgrave *Short Title Catalogue* (*STC*) of books printed in England from 1475 to 1640. For Power, microfilming began (in what he describes as a Eureka moment) with the idea that storing books on microfilm would allow for a print-on-demand business model, eliminating the need for expensive warehousing of physical books.[104] This idea then developed into the idea of a more purely microfilm-based project. To understand this process, I need to take one more step back and explain the history of the *STC*, and of its successor, the Wing catalogue, from 1641 to 1700, which was also the source for the continuation of the University Microfilm's project.

The *STC* was produced under the auspices of the Bibliographical Society and was edited by A. W. Pollard, whose views on facsimiles were discussed earlier, and G. R. Redgrave, who was a distinguished architect as well as a bibliographer. The catalogue was intended to record the publication of all books printed in England (and English books printed elsewhere) from 1475 to 1640. In his account of the Bibliographical Society, F. C. Francis described the catalogue as a publication that 'has revolutionized work on the books and printers of the period'.[105] In its first version, published in 1926, the catalogue contained 26,000 entries – it continued to be revised and expanded, and in its 1966 iteration, revised by Katharine F. Pantzer, it had 10,000 more items added, though many of these were further editions, rather than new titles.[106] Donald Wing produced a companion catalogue to take the list of books up to 1700, which was published in 1951.

Eugene Power's microfilm project, which took the Pollard and Redgrave *STC* as a starting point, could be seen in the terms I have been

---

[104] Eugene B. Power, *Edition of One: The Autobiography of Eugene B. Power Founder of University Microfilms* (Ann Arbor, MI: University Microfilms, 1990), p. 27.

[105] *The Bibliographical Society 1892–1942* (London: Bibliographical Society, 1949), p. 17.

[106] See the excellent summary of the changes in Paul S. Koda, 'The Revised *Short Title Catalogue* (*STC*): A Review Article', *Library Quarterly* 48 (1978): 306–9.

exploring here as the largest ever compilation of facsimiles.[107] From its inception, the project was an exercise both in access and in preservation. In terms of access, it continued the idea behind facsimile projects I have discussed, such as the Malone Society series, or facsimiles of the first folio. Because Power was American, and established an association with a number of American libraries, his notion of access included American access to early modern books housed in the great English research libraries, principally the British Library (or, as it was when Power's project began, the British Museum) and the Bodleian Library.[108] In terms of preservation, libraries were from the beginning interested in the way that microfilms of their rare book holdings would limit the need for scholars to handle the books; this idea was reinforced during the Second World War, when English (and European) libraries were very conscious of how easily books could be destroyed.[109] Indeed, the British Library still lists past holdings of rare books that were destroyed or damaged in the Blitz of World War II. When the war began, Power obtained a large Rockefeller grant to increase the speed with which he could preserve books in England by microfilming them. The development of this more sophisticated and resilient microfilming process was shaped by the war even more profoundly, because Power was also engaged in the filming of secret documents of various kinds for the American Office of the Coordinator of Information. As Bonnie Mak points out, the two aspects of Power's activities intersected, in the end, since the intelligence work allowed University Microfilms to use the most advanced photographic equipment available at the time for the Early English Books project.[110]

It is important to note that, from the start, the microfilm series was not systematic but was, in many respects, shaped by the availability of source material as the photographic process was undertaken in different libraries.

---

[107] See Power, *Edition of One*, p. 95.   [108] Ibid., p. 93.

[109] For a useful brief account, see the Folgerpedia entry 'History of *Early English Books Online*' (https://folgerpedia.folger.edu/History_of_Early_English_Books_Online?_ga=2.206480723.1104537303.1653788361-1926339928.1653455100, accessed 29 May 2022).

[110] Bonnie Mak, 'Archaeology of a Digitization', *Journal of the Association of Information Science and Technology* 65 (2014): 1518; and see Power's own account, *Edition of One*, pp. 134–7.

Power began by filming in England, although books from American libraries such as the Huntington were eventually included. Most microfilm reels contained a somewhat random collection of around thirty books (books were photographed according to their availability in particular libraries, rather than in any order of publication date or *STC* reference number). While there have been a number of quite critical analyses of the results of the University Microfilms project, some of which I will discuss in more detail later in this Element, it is worth acknowledging the enormous enhancement of research opportunities created by the project, especially for scholars who might be seen as hampered by limited or non-existent access to a research library like the British Library. While Power may have begun by seeing the project as a way to enhance access from within American research libraries that did not have the kind of extensive holdings found in the British Library, the nature of microfilm meant that sets could be reprinted many times over and sent out far and wide, including, I might say, to Australia, where I made extensive use of them as an honours student writing a thesis on Elizabethan fiction in 1975. However, cost remained a significant factor in limiting access, so that, for example, in Melbourne, where I studied, only one of five universities had subscribed to the microfilm series.[111] After an initial production of one book per reel, the individual microfilm reels soon contained a range of books, so that they had to be cross-indexed to the *STC*.[112] Because the individual items appeared in random order in random microfilm reels, in order to find a specific book a reader needed to locate its entry in the *STC*, then turn to the printed index that indicated which reel and item number corresponded to particular *STC* number.

Because of the impetus provided by the war both to University Microfilm's intelligence work, and to the Early English Books project, the filming of books proceeded at an enhanced rate. Eventually the series was to include copies of books held in American libraries, and as the *STC* and

---

[111] Cost for access continued to be a factor in relation to the digitization of the series, as I discuss in what follows.

[112] For an especially sophisticated analysis of the relationship between *EEBO* and its microfilm source, and the way that source was constructed, see Mak, 'Archaeology of a Digitization', pp. 1515–26.

Wing catalogues themselves were revised and expanded, so the microfilm series expanded to take that into account. By the mid 1960s, the microfilm series had reached close to three million pages.[113] The comprehensiveness of the series was extremely important, but this revolution in access did not come without compromises, as we have seen to be the case with all facsimiles. The most dramatic shift was from three dimensions to two. Previous photographic facsimiles were, like their originals, books (specifically codices), or contained within books. Microfilm as a medium represented a dramatic shift from the book to the image, and this had some significant consequences for the nature of the facsimile as a process, as opposed to a finished product. Put succinctly, microfilm encourages the reader to see the book as a series of individual images of pages or openings (pairs of pages) that flow past. A microfilm is a scroll, rather than a codex, and is read through scrolling in an anticipation of the way that digital text on a computer is scrolled through rather than paged through. There is absolutely no real sense of the size of the original, even if its dimensions are given at the beginning of the images, which was usually the case with the microfilms. Books of all formats (octavo, quarto, folio) appear to be roughly the same size when viewed using the UMI images. And, as with the Hinman first folio facsimile, the images are in black and white, not colour.

As with all facsimiles, convenience and authenticity are here again in tension with each other.[114] As microfilm, the UMI Early Book series was hardly easy to use. In a fascinating essay, Zachary Lesser describes how the University of Pennsylvania decided in the late 1960s, at considerable cost, to order a set of bound photocopies of the Early English Books series.[115] This can be seen as a lingering distrust of a facsimile that was too far removed from the three-dimensionality of the original, and in many respects, as

---

[113] See Stevens Rice, 'University Microfilms', *Reference Quarterly* 6 (1966): 16.

[114] For a careful analysis of the utility and drawbacks of facsimiles from a bibliographical perspective, see G. Thomas Tanselle, 'Reproductions and Scholarship', in *Literature and Artifacts* (Charlottesville: Bibliographical Society of the University of Virginia, 1998), pp. 60–88.

[115] Zachary Lesser, 'Xeroxing the Renaissance: The Material Text of Early Modern Studies', *Shakespeare Quarterly* 70 (2019): 3 31.

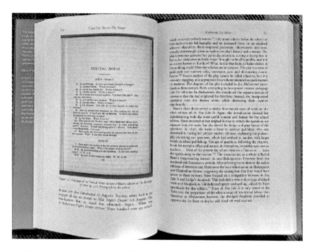

Figure 36 Opening from Molly G. Yarn, *Shakespeare's 'Lady Editors':
A New History of the Shakespearean Text* (Cambridge: Cambridge
University Press, 2022)

Lesser explains, simply housing these xeroxed books in a dedicated room, which allowed, for example, graduate students to browse in a way that would normally not be possible with an actual rare book collection, recreated the experience of work within a dedicated research library. In a way, the xeroxed books represent a further stage of mediation, since the microfilm process turns a book with gatherings of pages into a set of double page images, so that we do not see the recto (front) and verso (back) of a single page, but rather we see the opened pair of pages which are the verso on the left and the recto of the next page on the right.[116] We can see this from any photograph of an open book (Figure 36).

Lesser explains that the process of xeroxing from microfilm involved a continuous roll of paper, and to create the 'pages' of a book, pairs with

---

[116] As explained by Lesser, ibid., pp. 17–20.

blank sides were folded against each other, so that what in the original was a recto page became a verso page, and vice versa. Lesser sums up with an observation that is especially helpful for understanding the way that a facsimile needs to be seen through the perspective of utility, rather than an aesthetically driven desire for authenticity: 'The Xerox books offer the outward appearance of reproducing the early modern book "in virtual facsimile", but in fact what they make available is the *text* of the book in an approximation of its early printed form.'[117] Those at the University of Pennsylvania who hankered after something at least approaching the physical form of a book were right in seeing the difficulties of engaging at any length of time with the form of the microfilm. Looking back from today, however, we can see the microfilm series as a stage in a development that brought facsimiles into the digital age.

7 The Resilience of Books and the Resurrection of Old Editions

Before turning, finally, to the advent of digital facsimiles, I want to take a brief detour into the continuing market for facsimiles of early modern texts produced as 'modern' books, and to acknowledge the remarkable repackaging in facsimile form of nineteenth-century editions of early modern writers. Both these endeavours relate to the way that facsimiles played (and continue to play) a significant part in the opening up of the historicist study of early modern writing. The broadening of the canon from a relatively narrow group of writers was facilitated by increased access via facsimiles to writing by less well-known literary figures, as well as to print genres like pamphlets, ballads, and newsbooks that were previously passed over as subliterary. Not only literary scholars but also historians engaged in this more detailed encounter with the enormous bulk of printed material from the fifteenth to the eighteenth centuries. Writing published only in manuscript also came to be included in this 'moment of the facsimile'.

---

[117] Ibid., p. 24; and see Lisa Gitelman's fascinating analysis of the political and cultural implications of xeroxing in her *Paper Knowledge: Towards a Media History of Documents* (Durham, NC: Duke University Press, 2014), chapter 3.

Figure 37 Three examples of Scolar Press facsimiles

For literary scholars working towards an expanded (if not entirely revolutionary) canon, the most attractive albeit short-lived facsimile series was produced by Scolar Press between 1967 and 1972. Scolar Press was founded by the bibliographer Robin Alston and published a large range of facsimiles of mainly seventeenth-century printed literary works by authors ranging from Milton and Donne through to more obscure figures (back then) like Margaret Cavendish.[118] Available at an affordable price in paperback as well as hardback, but printed on good-quality paper, these facsimiles were reasonably durable and a pleasure to use. One notable feature of the series was that Alston designed the facsimiles to approximate their original size (see Figure 37).

Scolar Press produced hundreds of facsimiles, but they went out of print quite quickly and did not have the impact they perhaps should have had. However, more recent times have seen the return of Power/University Microfilm's idea of print-on-demand facsimiles through a scheme known as the BiblioLife network, which also engages in the practice of reprinting nineteenth-century editions. The print-on-demand service from BiblioLife and its associated presses has offered print versions of a large number of Early

[118] See ODNB Alston, Robin.

Figure 38 BiblioLife *Hamlet* reprint

English Books titles in a process that is an advance on the xeroxing process discussed earlier, so that the buyer receives a bound book, albeit one which, because of the transformation of microfilm image back into print, reverses recto and verso in the same way that Lesser describes as the situation with the University of Pennsylvania's xeroxes (see Figure 38).

Early English Books Online, now owned by ProQuest, has made available an increasing number of titles for this print-on-demand process. In a foundational analysis of this phenomenon, Whitney Trettien uses the fortuitous example of a reprinted version of Milton's *Areopagitica*.[119] She

---

[119] Whitney Trettien, 'A Deep History of Electronic Textuality: The Case of *English Reprints Jhon* [sic] *Milton Areopagitica*', *Digital Humanities Quarterly* 7 (2013): 1–23.

points out that *Areopagitica* is an especially apt example of this publishing practice because Milton's discussion of books, ideas, and censorship contains, in Trettien's words, a 'vital materialist theory of mediation'.[120] Milton believed, after all, that ideas escape any material suppression of their container. Trettien traces print-on-demand reproductions of texts such as Milton's back to the nineteenth-century popular yet quasi-antiquarian editions. While a number of print-on-demand books can be traced back to digitized versions of scanned early modern originals, Trettien notes that many of them are in fact reprints of those nineteenth-century editions, many of which have been scanned and made available via Google Books.

These print-on-demand and Google Books facsimiles were preceded, in the 1960s and 1970s, by a series of reprints/facsimiles of nineteenth-century editions produced by several especially prolific editors, particularly from the mid-to-late nineteenth century. Such volumes allowed scholars to work on a greater range of literary material, following on from the significantly expanded canon these earlier editors had been instrumental in creating.[121] These editions had gone out of favour by the mid-twentieth century, derided as amateurish by the new breed of editors brought up on New Bibliographical methods. In the 1960s, however, the complete works of several early modern authors remained without modern editions, and two presses stepped in to produce facsimiles of the nineteenth-century editions of these authors' writings. The publishers were able to capitalize on the fact that all of these works were out of copyright, so it cost publishers nothing (in terms of rights or permissions or royalties) to republish them. These reprints were especially influential where libraries were not subscribing to the University Microfilm Early English Books series because of the relatively high cost and, in the case of many universities, low demand. Both of the presses that made nineteenth-century editions newly available were American: Russell & Russell, founded by Sidney Russell and in operation until the 1990s, and AMS Press (American Magazine Service). Both publishers used photographic processes to create facsimile books: AMS published

---

[120] Ibid., p. 4.

[121] For a detailed account of this nineteenth-century editing, see Salzman, *Editors Construct the Renaissance Canon*.

Alexander Grosart's late nineteenth-century editions of Sylvester, Greville, Breton, Marvell, Cowley, Quarles, and Davies, while Russell & Russell published his editions of Greene and Dekker.

Other presses also engaged in this process in the 1960s, including Phaeton Press, which published Montague Summers's 1915 edition of Aphra Behn in 1967. These are, of course, facsimiles of editions, as opposed to the facsimiles of original texts which I have otherwise been discussing. However, they attest to the increasing interest in what we might call the totality of early modern writing, which was addressed in one way by the University Microfilm Project. One significant gap in the nineteenth-century editions available for facsimile reproduction in the twentieth century was the work of women writers, especially from the seventeenth century. This gap was filled, at least in part, by a highly influential print facsimile series, *The Early Modern Englishwoman*, published by Ashgate with the first volumes appearing in 1996. These volumes were edited by a roll call of scholars instrumental in rediscovering early modern women writers, and they included facsimiles invaluable to the project of canon expansion, such as the copy of Mary Wroth's *Urania*, edited by the pioneering Wroth scholar Josephine A. Roberts and which included Wroth's own hand-written corrections.[122] These were uncorrected photographic facsimiles of individual copies, with introductions by scholars like Roberts. This growing series, like the Scolar Press run of facsimiles, showed that a market remained for what we might call more traditional, printed versions of facsimiles.

Another substantial gap in the University Microfilms project was the fact that it covered only print, not the enormous body of writing from the period that was produced and circulated in manuscript form, which greatly reduced the presence of women writers. Some projects from around this time did begin to address this disparity of access, again through a microfilm facsimile process. Major examples dating from the 1990s include the Adam Matthew microfilm collection of Katherine Philips manuscripts, now available in digital form.[123] Indeed, this ongoing desire for access to the cornucopia of

---

[122] Josephine A. Roberts, ed., Mary Wroth, *Urania*. The Early Modern Englishwoman Series 1, part 1 (New York: Routledge, 1996).

[123] *Orinda: The Literary Manuscripts of Katherine Philips*, Adam Matthews, four microfilm reels.

primary early modern material was seen by many as 'solved' by the transformation of facsimiles into the digital realm.

8 Screen and Page: Digital Facsimiles

In step with the technological transformation of the 1990s, *Early English Books* 'went digital' in 1998. (As a point of reference, the first smartphone is generally agreed to be the IBM Simon of 1994.) While this can be seen as a process that simply involved shifting the way readers could access facsimiles of early modern printed books, it is best seen through the lens of remediation, as outlined in an influential article by Diana Kichuk on the emergence of the digital *EEBO* (or, *Early English Books Online*).[124] Remediation puns on 're-media', and is, as Kichuk explains, 'the re-presentation or re-purposing of old media in new media'.[125] *Early English Books Online* is the perfect example of this because it converted microfilmed images of early modern books into digital images. I have already discussed how the microfilm images bear an already mediated relationship to their originals: the microfilm images are in two dimensions, not three; they are black and white; they are images of opened, paired pages; they do not account for bindings and other physical features of the book object itself; and while rulers were often placed next to a page to give some idea of dimensions, all the various dimensions were compressed into the microfilm frame so that all books appear to be the same size.[126] Furthermore, images were sometimes cropped, blurred, double-exposed, and so on. Most of these issues were compounded by the very process of 'reading' (by which we usually really mean 'looking at') microfilm, with equipment that was awkward to use and that projected the film images onto screens with resolutions and light levels that strained the user's eyes and patience.

Chadwyck-Healey launched the first manifestation of the *EEBO* interface in 2003, and it represented a remarkable advance in reach and convenience over the microfilm series. This advantage begins with the search

---

[124] Diana Kichuk, 'Metamorphosis: Remediation in Early English Books Online (*EEBO*)', *Literary and Linguistic Computing* 22 (2007): 291–303.

[125] Ibid., p. 292. [126] See Lesser and Trettien, 'Material/Digital', pp. 402–23.

function. With the microfilm series, the user had to start with the *STC* or Wing entry, then use an index (in book form) to match the *STC* number to a microfilm reel number and reel position, then wind through the microfilm reel to locate the desired facsimile. *Early English Books Online* allowed for online searching – for title, author, date of publication, and so forth – much as one would search a library catalogue (and indeed eventually *EEBO* subscribers could list *EEBO* titles in their online catalogues so many users can now search for *EEBO* 'books' directly from their institution's library catalogues). Microfilm users had considerable access issues, given that microfilm readers were often hard to book in a library and were also often out of order; in contrast, *EEBO* delivered its images directly to the user's computer, so long as the user had access to a subscription. (It is worth noting that initially subscriptions to *EEBO* were extremely expensive, leaving many libraries, including my own at the time, unable to justify the cost until libraries began to negotiate group subscriptions and organizations like the Renaissance Society of America provided access for members.)

Early English Books Online has many affordances beyond just access, which I will address in more detail in what follows, but, at this point, it is still necessary to follow Kichuk into some sense of how this remediated facsimile of a facsimile compounded, at least in some ways, the limitations of the microfilm series. In order to allow for relatively fast downloads, *EEBO* had to reduce the already limited resolution of the microfilm images.[127] Kichuk offers this stern corrective to enthusiasts who overstate the connection between *EEBO* and early modern printed books: 'While digitization gives unprecedented access to content, that content is distorted by virtue of its production, and the print work it purports to represent with exactness, while seeming so tantalizingly accessible, is illusive [*sic*].'[128] In 2019, *EEBO* migrated to the ProQuest Platform. This too produced advantages as well as new issues of remediation. The ProQuest Platform allows an integration of the *EEBO* images with related material, principally

---

[127] For a more detailed and technical explanation, see Kichuk, 'Metamorphosis', pp. 294–5.

[128] Ibid., p. 296.

with transcriptions of the source texts directly aligned by the platform with the standard text. The transcriptions were created as a collaborative project entitled *EEBO-TCP* (or *Text Creation Partnership* (*TCP*)), which began in 1999. *Text Creation Partnership* allows the transcriptions of the source texts to be wholly searchable. For this functionality alone, *TCP* is an invaluable resource, even though users are not always aware of the limitations of the interface, and the transcriptions themselves, like all such further remediations, necessarily contain errors.[129] The texts can be downloaded as PDFs, but the ProQuest interface does make the experience even further removed from the experience of reading the original books: the ProQuest platform is more like a database than its predecessor (see Figures 39 and 40).

Like the microfilm series and the preceding Chadwyck-Healey *EEBO* platform, ProQuest is expensive, and if, as Bonnie Mak has explained, it is becoming a kind of default fundamental research tool for early modern and eighteenth-century studies, then there will be those who are excluded from its use if they work outside the kinds of institutions that can afford it.[130] At the same time there have been some fierce debates about the utility of *EEBO* as a compendium of facsimiles, given some of the drawbacks regarding image quality and user experience I have discussed. The creation of searchable texts through *TCP* increased the discussion around the value of this kind of database, although the transcribed material no longer bears any close relationship to the idea of a facsimile, however loosely that term might be used.

A few years ago, an illuminating discussion of this aspect of *EEBO-TCP* and its general value was staged in the pages of the journal *Textual Cultures*. The discussion focussed on the quantitative uses to which the database might be put, and so it moved away from the facsimile elements I have been considering in this book. Still, it touched on many issues relevant to the facsimile aspect of *EEBO*, notably the idea of representation, as opposed to the idea of imperfect duplication. Michael Gavin began the debate by arguing that the short title catalogues (*STC* and Wing) were already metadata, rather than compendia or the equivalent of library catalogue

---

[129] See, for example, Ian Gadd, 'The Use and Misuse of Early English Books Online', *Literature Compass* 6 (2009): 680–92.

[130] Mak, 'Archaeology of a Digitization', p. 1521.

Figure 39 Screenshot of the 'old' *EEBO* from Chadwyck-Healey (accessed WayBack Machine 30 June 2022)

entries.[131] For Gavin, the true value of *EEBO-TCP*, and even of its precursor, the microfilm series, is not to facilitate the reading of early modern editions, but to facilitate the gathering of data. This idea can be related to the fashionable notion of distant, as opposed to close, reading,

[131] Michael Gavin, 'How to Think about *EEBO*', *Textual Cultures* 11 (2017): 75.

Figure 40 Screenshot of the 'new' *EEBO* from ProQuest (accessed 30 June 2022). The column on the right has links to suggested critical essays; the image file can be downloaded as a PDF but so also can the *TCP* (i.e., transcribed text) file.

championed early on by Franco Moretti, amongst others.[132] Distant reading is rather different from the new textualist notion of looking at, rather than through, books and their avatars.[133] In a response to Gavin, Peter C. Herman counters the idea of linked, distributed, and (one might say) de-individualized data with the microfilm/*EEBO* experience of the historically oriented scholar wanting access to primary source material that remains hard to reach in its original form but still yields considerable knowledge through facsimiles or even facsimiles of facsimiles. Herman sums up his own experience of research using *EEBO*: '[T]he effect is not greater abstraction, but greater specificity.'[134] Recently, Zachary Lesser and Whitney Trettien have argued for a new, digitally literate bibliography, using a specific example, and concluded: 'Only when we approached the digital copy as a textual object in its own right, rather than as a bookish facsimile, could we properly see the evidence it offered towards understanding its own production.'[135]

This idea is part of the shift towards greater opportunities for the kind of historically oriented analysis of early modern writing that relies on some form of access to the fullest possible range of that writing: access best provided to the world at large by facsimiles. Implications of the increased access provided by not only *EEBO*, but the increasing range of smaller facsimile series, often of manuscript material, can be illuminated by returning to a debate over editing. This particular debate followed on from reactions against the 'ideal' text that was a result of the way that New Bibliography conceived of the editorial task.

9 New Textualism and the Exploded Original

In my earlier discussion of the New Bibliography, I explained (granted, in a simplified way) that when editors influenced by New Bibliographic

---

[132] Franco Moretti, *Distant Reading* (London: Verso, 2013).

[133] See Margreta de Grazia and Peter Stallybrass, 'The Materiality of the Shakespearean Text', *Shakespeare Quarterly* 44 (1993), pp. 256–7.

[134] Peter C. Herman, '*EEBO* and Me', *Textual Cultures* 13 (2020): 211.

[135] Lesser and Trettien, 'Material/Digital', p. 419.

methods worked with a number of primary source texts, such as the first and second quartos of *Hamlet* and the folio text (all substantially different), they worked towards a single, 'ideal' text, either to recreate (to the best of their abilities) what the author intended, or to capture a single but inaccessible manuscript source text. In the 1980s, partly in reaction to this quest for textual origins, a number of editors and scholars argued that, in cases like the works of Shakespeare where there was no 'original' manuscript source, the available primary texts should not be merged.[136] At the practical level, this resulted in editors producing separate texts of, say, the folio and quarto versions of *King Lear* (hence the name 'new textualism' often given to this approach).[137] At the theoretical level, this approach led to what was famously called 'un-editing' in an influential 1981 article by Randall McLeod.[138] Facsimiles play a vital role in McLeod's fundamental argument: that we need to pay close attention to the individual nature of early modern texts, to look *at* them, not *through* them. McLeod's essay, like so much of his writing, is copiously illustrated with facsimile extracts from the texts he discusses, because he keeps calling attention to the kinds of physical details in them that so much criticism, even textual criticism, either misses, or glosses over as unimportant.

Perhaps McLeod's most bravura performance of this is in his extraordinary discussion of George Herbert's poem 'Easter Wings'.[139] 'Easter Wings' is a concrete (i.e., shape) poem, but its appearance was reshaped every time it reappeared in an edition. McLeod (writing as Random Cloud)

---

[136] This is a complex subject but for my purposes best summed up in Egan, *Struggle for Shakespeare's Text*, chapter 4, and, for a more sympathetic account, see de Grazia and Stallybrass, 'The Materiality of the Shakespearean Text', pp. 255–83.

[137] For an influential example, see the essays in Gary Taylor and Michael Warren, eds., *The Division of the Kingdoms: Shakespeare's Two Versions of 'King Lear'* (Oxford: Clarendon, 1986).

[138] Randall McLeod, 'Un "Editing" Shak-speare', *SubStance* 10/11 (1981/82): 26–55. See also the discussion of a number of early modern examples in Leah Marcus, *Unediting the Renaissance: Shakespeare, Marlowe and Milton* (London: Routledge, 1996).

[139] Random Cloud, 'FIAT *f*LUX', in Randall M Leod, ed., *Crisis in Editing: Texts of the English Renaissance* (New York: AMS Press, 1994), 61–172.

keeps drawing our attention to slips, realignings, marks on paper, paper, including within the sometimes deliberately misnumbered pages of his essay. Again, this argument requires McLeod to reproduce as images the texts and re-textualizations he is discussing. Where might this lead in terms of facsimiles and editing? True un-editing would value the original over the edited text, and, given difficulties of accessing originals, would value the facsimile over the edited text. In that sense, *EEBO* might seem like the dream of the un-editing movement, but it cannot be. Not only is it a re-mediation, as discussed earlier, but as McLeod and others keep noting, each early modern printed book (i.e., every copy that makes up an edition) is unique. For *EEBO* truly to capture the textual condition of early modern books, we would need it – or any other set of facsimiles – to give us *every* instance, not just one exemplar, of *every* preserved early modern work. This unreachable goal, because of the digitization costs involved and the number of early modern texts in private hands, is perhaps a fever-dream that has occurred only to those devoted to Shakespeare.[140]

10 Endless Facsimiles and the Shakespeare Original(s)

Hinman's extraordinary effort to collate individual copies of the Shakespeare first folio may have yielded many insights into the process of printing it, but he turned up a rather disappointing number of variants from copy to copy. From that perspective, anyone other than an editor of Shakespeare might, as I have noted, question whether much would be gained by facsimiles of individual copies, in contrast to the Hinman facsimile, which, as already discussed, is patched together from a variety of 'best' pages. Might even the most fervent of 'un-editors' baulk at the thought of fifty facsimiles, let alone facsimiles of all 228 copies of the first folio that are extant?[141] The answer to this, at least in relation

---

[140] But see the 'Reassembling Marlowe' project, which has at least the aim of tracing individual surviving copies of Marlowe's works and where possible establishing their individual characteristics (https://reassemblingmarlowe.org/site).

[141] This is the number listed by the Shakespeare census (https://shakespearecensus .org/copy/149). The census notes that currently forty-two copies are available as digital facsimiles.

again to Shakespeare, is less concerned with printing history than it is with the impact of book history and studies of readers' responses to books, and to the transmission of those thoughts and interactions. In other words, facsimiles of copies stand to make the multifaceted modes of textual reception (rather than production) more accessible than ever before. The most dramatic recent example of this is a copy of the first folio in the Free Library of Philadelphia. This copy was largely ignored until Claire Bourne published an essay on its marginalia (with plenty of pictures), which led to speculation by Jason Scott-Warren that the annotator was John Milton.[142] After the considerable publicity this discovery stimulated, the library decided to produce a digital facsimile of the entire book.[143]

This is the most dramatic example of an annotated copy, and not all surviving copies have annotations or marginalia, but they all carry marks, changes, and other physical attributes that reveal clues about their journeys from their first appearance through to the present day. One might therefore well wish for a facsimile of every single one from the perspective of book history, or material culture, or even just from the perspective of the curiosity aroused by the knowledge that books travel through time and space. The number of online facsimiles of first folios is increasing, and the quality of what we can see is improving. A good example is the recent digitization of the Bodleian Library first folio which, like the one at the Free Library of Philadelphia, can be viewed and navigated in a number of different ways, and is captured in high resolution.[144] The Folger Shakespeare Library provides a similarly high-quality experience for a considerable proportion of its first folios. This can be compared to the situation only a few years ago when digital facsimiles were closer to the quality of the images on *EEBO* (though at least many non-*EEBO* facsimiles were usually in colour).

---

[142] Claire M. L. Bourne, 'Vide Supplementum: Early Modern Collation as Play-Reading in the First Folio', in Katherine Acheson, ed., *Early Modern English Marginalia* (London: Routledge, 2018), 195–233.

[143] Downloadable from the Free Library of Philadelphia's website (https://libwww.freelibrary.org/digital/feature/first-folio, accessed 29 June 2022).

[144] https://firstfolio.bodleian.ox.ac.uk, accessed 30 June 2022.

Figure 41 www.quartos.org, accessed 30 June 2022

However, even the trump card of Shakespeare cannot necessarily guarantee the protection of digital projects from the entropy that is so prevalent in the digital world. It is possible to view all of the British Library's collection of 142 Shakespeare quartos published before 1642, but the more ambitious project that aimed to capture a much larger range of quarto copies from six major libraries can no longer be accessed (see Figure 41).[145]

Despite the always looming obsolescence of many platforms that house digital facsimiles, there are now an increasing number of facsimiles (with drama predominating) that can be added to *EEBO* as resources not just for scholarship, but also for teaching, and as windows for the general public into the rich diversity of early modern books and manuscripts.[146]

From what we might call a theoretical point of view, this digital proliferation of facsimiles has coincided with an increasing scholarly emphasis on the physical nature of individual early modern books and manuscripts. The material turn in early modern studies has crashed into the digital era. The history of facsimiles I have been exploring here provides

---

[145] www.bl.uk/treasures/shakespeare/homepage.html, accessed 17 August 2022.

[146] Reliable sources of facsimiles include the Folger Shakespeare Library, the University of Victoria (Canada), and the Harry Ransom Center. For a convenient list, see Claire M. L. Bourne, 'Of Pilcrows' (www.ofpilcrows.com/resources-early-modern-plays-page-and-stage, accessed 30 June 2022).

a context for the tensions between material/immaterial books, given that facsimiles call our attention to the slippage between original and copy, authentic and inauthentic. A type-facsimile like Smeaton's *Solimon and Perseda* approximates the tactile experience of handling an early modern book, while a digital facsimile takes us the farthest possible distance from that experience. In a prescient article published in *Shakespeare Quarterly* in 2001, Jonathan Gil Harris offered a sophisticated critique of the desire for materiality that was prevalent in early modern studies during the 1990s.[147] Harris does this via an account of a purported lock of Shakespeare's hair, which played a part in the series of Shakespeare forgeries undertaken by Samuel Ireland and his son William Henry Ireland in the late eighteenth century. Harris notes that it is a mistake to posit a frozen essence that allows a historical object like 'Shakespeare's' hair to confer a version of time travel, but rather, he writes, such an object needs to be seen as standing for 'the ongoing process of location and dislocation'; or, in other words, these objects are part of a process of transmission.[148]

For my purposes, it is fortuitous that Harris uses the Ireland case as his example of the desire for the material object because the Ireland forgeries are tied to the way that the practical value of facsimiles shifted through the eighteenth century and into the nineteenth. With the Ireland forgeries, as with Shakespeare's hair, we are at the heart of the desire for authenticity, for closer access to originals – a need which allows for the facsimile, like the forgery, to insinuate itself into a chain of substitutes, which in turn calls into question the very nature of what an 'original' might be. As it turns out, facsimiles allowed Ireland to claim authenticity in the first place: not only did Ireland invent entire 'lost' Shakespeare texts (he wrote a play called *Vortigern* which now seems so obviously fake, but which was going to be performed as Shakespeare's just before Ireland's forgeries were exposed), but he forged Shakespeare's signature by tracing over the facsimiles of Shakespeare's 'authentic' signatures, which

---

[147] Jonathan Gil Harris, 'Shakespeare's Hair: Staging the Object of Material Culture', *Shakespeare Quarterly* 52 (2001): 479–91.

[148] Ibid., p. 482. See also Lesser, *Ghosts, Holes, Rips and Scrapes* for more on the 'Longue Durée' of books.

Figure 42 William Henry Ireland: Forged Shakespeare letter to Anne
Hathaway with signature, Huntington Library

Edmond Malone had recently produced as part of his edition of Shakespeare
(see Figure 42).[149]

As Alan Stewart notes in his account of the symbiotic relationship
between Ireland and Malone, the facsimile is at the heart of the process of
attempts to separate the authentic from the inauthentic.[150] As Stewart points
out, the Malone facsimiles of Shakespeare's signature were 'corrected' via
the engraving process, even if they were 'good enough' to assist in the
lengthy book Malone produced, which undermined the claim to authenticity
of the Ireland 'Shakespeare' material (see Figure 43).[151]

From this perspective, it is, I think, possible to address the tension
between the important work that is being undertaken on the material
book/manuscript and its use, and the proliferation of digital facsimiles.
There are many aspects of the knowledge brought to the early modern
period by the material history of books and manuscripts that require the

---

[149] For succinct accounts of the Ireland affair, see Jack Lynch, 'William Henry
Ireland's Authentic Forgeries', *Princeton University Library Chronicle* 66 (2004):
79–96; Robert Miles, 'Trouble in the Republic of Letters: The Reception of the
Shakespeare Forgeries', *Studies in Romanticism* 44 (2005): 317–40.

[150] Alan Stewart, 'Early Modern Lives in Facsimile', *Textual Practice* 23 (2009):
289–305.

[151] Ibid., pp. 299–300. Malone's book is *An Inquiry into the Authenticity of Certain
Miscellaneous Papers and Legal Instruments* (1796).

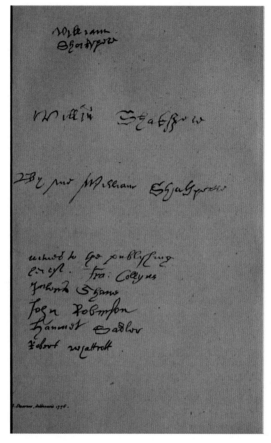

Figure 43 Edmond Malone, ed., *The Plays and Poems of Shakespeare*, vol. 1 (1790), facing p. 190, State Library of Victoria

book itself, so to speak. The context for such knowledge is also greatly enhanced by the access to facsimiles, which grow in number and sophistication with every iteration. Physical manuscripts and rare books require preservation, even from scholars, let alone the general public, and facsimiles can offer a way round the tension between preservation and access. It is also important to recognize all the aspects of access (and restriction) which have taken on a particular urgency at the time of writing this Element. It is to this issue that I now, finally, turn.

Coda

Covid-19

I have already mentioned how important facsimiles were for me when I was a student in Melbourne, Australia, working on the obscure topic of Elizabethan prose fiction. Working on prose fiction, and then on early modern women's writing, has been a lesson in seeing the centre (or the canon) from the margins, just as my geographical position has often felt like a similar handicap. Like many other areas of the humanities, early modern studies and Shakespeare studies have had to come to terms with the fact that they have often been dominated by an unacknowledged process of gatekeeping. The closed doors have been prised open, if only a little way, by approaches such as critical race studies.[152] It would be presumptuous to think of the affordances of digital facsimiles as having the same effect, but for all their limitations, facsimiles have allowed greater access to primary sources for early modern studies for more people who have, for a variety of reasons, found that the doors of the great research libraries were closed to them, or were too far distant.

I began work on this project in 2018 in the British Library, accustomed as I was to travel to England or America to undertake my research. Then the Covid-19 pandemic arrived and reminded those of us at a distance from major research hubs just how distant we were, only to realize that the doors were shut even to those who lived only a few blocks away from one. I was able to continue work on this project, in part, because of the quite amazing resources of the State Library of Victoria, but I could not have written this Element without using facsimiles. During the pandemic, scholars who were distant from

---

[152] For a useful summary of what is now a large and growing body of work, see Ruben Espinosa, 'Diversifying Shakespeare', *Literature Compass* 13 (2016): 58–68; and the special issue of *New Literary History* on Race and Periodization, 52.3/4 (2021) edited by Urvashi Chakravarty and Ayanna Thompson.

research libraries, who were in lockdown, who were in precarious employment or unemployed, managed to undertake research thanks to facsimiles, not just of primary material, but also of secondary sources, especially those from the nineteenth and early twentieth centuries via repositories such as Internet Archive and HathiTrust. This is not to diminish the requirement of many projects still to explore 'real' books, with all their attendant haptic details like paper thickness, binding quality, marginalia too faint to be picked up by photography, and so on. However, just as circumstances have conspired to separate us from each other and from our source material, so facsimiles and the digital world have, at least to some degree, overcome distance and brought us back together.

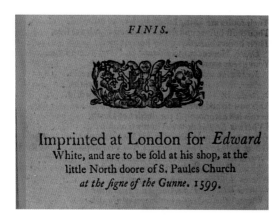

Or do I mean:

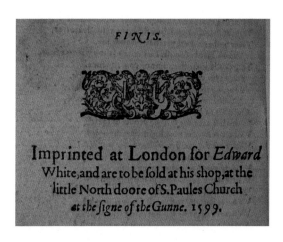

FINIS.

Imprinted at London for *Edward* White, and are to be sold at his shop, at the little North doore of S. Paules Church at the signe of the Gunne. 1599.

Glossary

In this study, I discuss a number of different kinds of facsimile. Here is a handy list of definitions of them:

Collotype facsimile: The collotype is a kind of photographic printing process invented in 1855.
    It allows for finer and more detailed reproduction because it does not use halftone screens to develop the image.

Hand-drawn facsimile: This usually involves tracing but the tracing is done by hand directly onto an individual page or portion of a page.

Photographic facsimile: Not long after the advent of photography, the Ordnance Survey Office in England experimented with various photographic reproductions before printing the first 162 pages of the 1623 Shakespeare folio in 1861. The quality of photographic facsimiles could vary considerably according to the type of equipment (and skill) used. In a photographic facsimile, as in a traced lithographic facsimile, the text or page might be 'improved' through the deletion of later marginal comments, or through clarifying blurred or broken type images, or even through emendation where the facsimilist thinks there has been an error in the original.

Traced facsimile: Usually, for a traced facsimile either the text is traced onto paper and then transferred to a stone to be printed using lithography, a process invented in the late eighteenth century which involves using a kind of crayon on a stone surface, which could then be printed from using rolled-on ink and paper. For single pages or parts of a page, the tracing might be done individually. That is, a page or section of a page in the 'original' copy might be traced and then reproduced to replace a damaged or missing page in another copy.

Type-facsimile: Here, a printer either uses type that has been preserved from an original printing process, or uses type that bears a close resemblance to the original type-face, or has new type cast to replicate the original type-face.

Acknowledgements

Librarians are the all too often unsung heroes of research, and for this particular project, they were more vital than ever, given the restrictions of the Covid-19 pandemic. I owe special thanks to Anna Welch and Des Cowley at the State Library of Victoria, Christian Algar at the British Library, Abbie Weinberg at the Folger Shakespeare Library, and Aaron T. Pratt at The Harry Ransom Center. The Inter-library Loan staff at La Trobe University's library were exceptionally helpful in response to many urgent requests. I also had help of various kinds from numbers of academics, both via Twitter, a platform to which I am somewhat addicted, and through emailed pleading. Thanks are particularly owed to David McInnis and to Zachary Lesser, who outed himself as a reviewer and who offered an extraordinarily detailed set of suggestions to improve the manuscript, all of which I have followed with immense gratitude. The two general editors of this series, Rory Loughnane and Claire Bourne, offered invaluable, detailed suggestions and considerable encouragement. This little Element was written in a very crowded house that suffered a number of (necessary) Covid-19 lockdowns, so I owe a great deal to Susan, Imogen, Joseph, and Charles, for their love and tolerance.

Cambridge Elements ≡

Shakespeare and Text

Claire M. L. Bourne

The Pennsylvania State University

Claire M. L. Bourne is Associate Professor of English at The Pennsylvania State University. She is author of *Typographies of Performance in Early Modern England* (Oxford University Press 2020) and editor of the collection *Shakespeare / Text* (Bloomsbury 2021). She has published extensively on early modern book design and reading practices in venues such as *PBSA*, *ELR*, *Shakespeare*, and numerous edited collections. She is also co-author (with Jason Scott-Warren) of an article attributing the annotations in the Free Library of Philadelphia's copy of the Shakespeare First Folio to John Milton. She has edited Fletcher and Massinger's *The Sea Voyage* for the *Routledge Anthology of Early Modern Drama* (2020) and is working on an edition of *Henry the Sixth, Part 1* for the Arden Shakespeare, Fourth Series.

Rory Loughnane

University of Kent

Rory Loughnane is Reader in Early Modern Studies and Co-director of the Centre for Medieval and Early Modern Studies at the University of Kent. He is the author or editor of nine books and has published widely on Shakespeare and textual studies. In his role as Associate Editor of the New Oxford Shakespeare, he has edited more than ten of Shakespeare's plays, and co-authored with Gary Taylor a book-length study about the 'Canon and Chronology' of Shakespeare's works. He is a General Editor of the forthcoming

Oxford Marlowe edition, a Series Editor of Studies in Early Modern Authorship (Routledge), a General Editor of the *CADRE* database (cadredb.net), and a General Editor of The Revels Plays series (Manchester University Press).

About the Series

Cambridge Elements in Shakespeare and Text offers a platform for original scholarship about the creation, circulation, reception, remaking, use, performance, teaching, and translation of the Shakespearean text across time and place. The series seeks to publish research that challenges – and pushes beyond – the conventional parameters of Shakespeare and textual studies.

Cambridge Elements ≡

Shakespeare and Text

Printed in the United States
by Baker & Taylor Publisher Services